The Earth for Sam

by the same author

THE STARS FOR SAM

THE SEA FOR SAM
(with Wilfrid S. Bronson)

AND THAT'S WHY

THE SKY IS BLUE

AMERICA'S TREASURE

THE

Revised Edition

Edited by PAUL F. BRANDWEIN

Illustrated with photographs

Harcourt, Brace & World, Inc. NEW YORK

W. MAXWELL REED

Earth FOR SAM

Dedicated to my mother

EMILY PUTNAM REED

Editor's Note

The Earth for Sam is a story of the dramatic changes the earth, its plants, and animals have undergone over millions of years. The boy Sam heard the story first from his uncle, W. Maxwell Reed, a master storyteller.

Mr. Reed's original text has been revised; fresh material based on new research has been added. In assessing the new research, we have had the counsel of Mary Patsuris, of the American Museum of Natural History, whose help has been invaluable.

Every attempt has been made to retain the qualities that won for the story a favored place through the years with so many young people.

PAUL F. BRANDWEIN

Contents

The Earth for Sam

1

When the Earth Was Hot

A long, very long time ago, the earth was hot — so hot that the water boiled and the sky was full of steam. Nothing could live on account of the heat. There were no sea or land plants or animals on the earth.

In some places the rocks had melted and streams of thick white-hot lava flowed over the land and into the water. Of course, there was no one there to see the great clouds of steam that rose up to the sky when all this melted rock flowed into the sea.

The uprushing steam probably caused thunderstorms, so that the sky may have been full of lightning, and if anyone had been there, they would have heard loud roars of thunder nearly all the time.

The clouds were so thick that the sunlight never reached the earth. If you had been there, you would have found that most of the light came from flashes of lightning and from the white-hot molten rock that flowed over the land and into the boiling sea; and the roar of the thunder would have been deafening.

Besides the thunder that was roaring all the time, something else happened that would have been very dangerous if you had been there. Many meteors, or big shooting stars, rushed through the steaming air and struck the earth. They made even a louder noise rushing along than all the boiling oceans, and could be heard even above the thunder.

These shooting stars, many of which were as large as one of the big cities you see today, were white-hot. Because they were so hot, they were blindingly bright, and for a few seconds, just before they struck the earth or rushed into the ocean, they were reflected in the great clouds of steam until it looked as if the sun were shining among the clouds.

You know that sometimes when two rocks hit each other very hard, sparks are made. When these great shooting stars hit the earth, not only were there thousands of sparks, but also the very ground was melted, and the melted rock, white-hot like the stars themselves, splashed over everything. So hard did they strike the earth that even hills were thrown about as if they, as well as the rocks, were only pieces of mud, and for hundreds of miles the ground would shake and tremble.

When these shooting stars fell into the sea, they made great waves, higher than our big buildings, and these waves would dash over the shores, and melted rocks and water swirled as in a great storm. No animals or plants could have lived in the smother of steam hanging like a cloud over everything. Sometimes the steam, when it got high in the sky, would cool and turn into rain, but when the drops of water fell upon the hot rocks, they were again turned into steam.

Very, very slowly the rocks became cool and the clouds scattered so that the bright sunlight came down upon both the land and the water. The rain from the clouds was no longer turned into steam by the hot rocks. It reached the earth and flowed off the land in streams and rivers as it does today.

How do we know the earth formed in this way? Not a living

thing, not even a piece of seaweed, was anywhere on the earth at that time. However, for various reasons many men who have devoted their lives to the study of the earth think that it was formed in this way. Of course they may be wrong, for, after all, mankind has only just begun to discover the answer to these great questions. Some English scientists think the earth was formed in a somewhat different manner, and a number of American geologists and astronomers agree with them.

Their theory is that the earth was once a huge ball of melted liquid rock and that it was then about the same size as it is now. At that time there were no big shooting stars, for all the rock and iron had been used up in making that enormous ball of melted rock we call the earth.

Then slowly, very slowly, the earth began to cool. For a long time the crust of the earth was so hot that no water could stay on the surface — it was boiled and turned to steam and made huge clouds in the sky. Finally, as the land cooled and rain was possible, the water accumulated in the low places and the ponds grew into lakes. The oceans, on the other hand, formed early in huge basins, which developed as the earth cooled and hardened. The Pacific Ocean perhaps is in a basin formed, some astronomers think, when part of the earth was pulled out to make the moon. Whether this is quite true remains to be discovered. During all this time the lightning must have been blinding and the thunder deafening, but there was no living thing in all the earth to see or hear.

Or perhaps it happened in still another way; we do not know with certainty. We do seem to believe that the earth was once part of the sun — or at least of material that eventually formed the sun. Some think that the parts that were broken away from the sun at once formed millions of little bodies. From time to time these little bodies met in collision and kept falling together until finally the great ball we call the earth was formed.

On the other hand, some astronomers claim that the pieces of the sun, white-hot and fiery, almost at once formed a huge ball of melted rock — the earth.

And how was the earth material — and the material that formed the other planets — pulled out from the sun? It was once thought that another sun wandered close enough to our sun to pull out the material that formed the earth and the planets.

A more recent educated guess of the way the earth and the planets originated is stated by Whipple. Should you want to read it in his own words, he tells it in the *Scientific American,* May 1948, pp. 34-35. He assumes first that there was a huge dust cloud in space that begins to condense; this is the forerunner of the sun and the planets. Within this cloud are minor clouds. All of these clouds eventually condense.

The largest of the clouds will eventually form the sun while the minor clouds drift around the sun, collecting bits of other clouds. As they do so, they form protoplanets (beginning planets). Eventually the large cloud collapses and forms the sun; the minor clouds condense and form the planets.

Whichever educated guess you take as to the origin of the earth, there is agreement on this: in the beginning the earth was just very hot.

For years to come it may not be decided which of the present descriptions of the origin of the earth is correct. You may be sure, however, that during those years many will be working hard to find out the truth. The hunt for more knowledge about the history of the earth is even more interesting than reading about it after it has been discovered. As you read these chapters, you will find there are many important things we do not know. Perhaps some day you may assist the hunters for knowledge and add your bit to the known history of the earth.

Now a curious thing happened. Tiny living things appeared in the water, which was still warm even if it was not boiling. These living things were so small that if you had been there with a magnifying glass, you could not have seen them. They were floating around in the water of the ocean, but the sea was not as salty in those days as it is now. Perhaps these first signs of life were formed in the soft warm mud near the edge of some shallow sea.

Whatever they were, they were the only living creatures on the earth. The land was only rock and mud and there was not a blade of grass, not a flower, not a tree all over the earth — only jagged rocks. Here and there great streams of melted rock were still coming from below the ground. Now and then the land would be shaken by an explosion as some volcano would blow fire high into the air and send streams of white-hot melted lava down its sides.

In the beginning, the ocean must have been a very dangerous place for these first living things. They couldn't swim and they couldn't see — just little specks floating in the warm water, but so small you couldn't have seen them with a magnifying glass, or even with the most wonderful microscope that has ever been made.

Sometimes hundreds of them were carried by the swift currents in the ocean to some place where the hot lava was still coming up from the ground and making the water boil. The tiny specks of life couldn't endure boiling water any better than we can, so hundreds of them must have been killed by being scalded. Then, once in a while, large waves would carry them deep into the ocean where it was dark, because the sunlight couldn't get through so much water; these conditions might have killed them as well. In any event, there were always thousands of these little creatures floating near the surface of the ocean in the warm and sunny water in those times of long ago.

2

The Air We Breathe

If you had come to the earth in those days and tried to walk on the rocks, you would have suffocated. There was plenty of air, but even a dog would have panted for breath and then died, for the air was not good to breathe.

Before we go on and learn about the adventures of the first specks of life, let's try to find out about this air that we breathe and that was just as necessary to most of those early living things as it is to us. From now on we will call these first living things, these tiny specks of life, *protists*. They were the first living things, but they were neither plants nor animals. No one really knows how they appeared, but they must have been very tiny — tiny enough to be seen only by a powerful microscope.

In the first place, you look right through air and walk right through it, so that you have sometimes probably thought it was nothing. When you get into a strong wind, you realize the air has such force that it will almost blow you over. An electric bulb has no air in it. If you weigh one of these bulbs on some very good scales, so that the bulb on one side of the scale will just balance the weight on the other side, and then if you make a very tiny hole in the bulb to let in the air, you will find that the bulb weighs more. The side of the scale holding the bulb will go down, which shows that when you let in the air, you increased the weight of the bulb. Therefore, the air has weight — very little to be sure, but then there is a great deal of air, so that the total weight of all the air is very large. It is because air has weight that it is able sometimes to blow the branches off the trees and to make it hard for you to run against the wind.

The hardest thing of all is to understand just what air is. The air is made of millions of very little particles — so small that you cannot see them even with a microscope. When you go out in a strong wind, millions of these little particles blow against you and make it hard for you to walk. When millions of them blow against a branch of a tree with great force, they make the branch bend and swing from side to side until it begins to crack and then, perhaps, it will break and fall to the ground.

All these little particles are not alike. There are several kinds that are quite different from each other. You know there are many different kinds of dogs. Some dogs run very fast and won't come near you, while other dogs are very friendly and follow you everywhere. Most of the air we breathe is made of two kinds of particles, or atoms. One kind is called oxygen and the other kind is called nitrogen. If you can't remember the word oxygen, perhaps you can remember its scientific nickname, or symbol, O. This isn't the figure zero; it is the letter O. In the same way, the nickname for nitrogen is N. Those who don't know atoms very well call them oxygen and nitrogen, but those who are well acquainted with atoms call them O and N. In air, oxygen doesn't travel alone; it joins with another atom of oxygen (O) to form a molecule of oxygen. We write this O_2. Similarly, nitrogen (N) joins with another atom (N) to form N_2. Both the oxygen (O_2) and the nitrogen (N_2) are gases.

These gases are just as different as the two kinds of dogs we just described. O_2 is a very friendly gas and likes to join other atoms and go with them, while N_2 likes to be by itself and is very slow to join with other atoms. The sociable gas O_2 is very valuable to us, for it is the gas that keeps us alive when we breathe. We cannot live unless we are breathing O_2 all the time. Animals and plants must have O_2 all the time or else they die. Of course, the O_2 is part of the air.

There is another very funny set of atoms called carbon, whose nickname is C, and this is the last set of atoms that you will have to remember for a long time. These atoms behave in a very strange way. A diamond is pure carbon (C); also coal is C. Some day you will learn why these two things both made of C look so different. When coal, or wood, which have a lot of carbon (C) in them, burn, they join with oxygen to form a new gas called carbon dioxide or CO_2. This name shows just what the gas is made of, for it says there are one atom of carbon and two atoms of oxygen. You write the 2 a little below the line and after the O to show that two of the atoms of O joined the one atom of C — thus CO_2. Remember, just as carbon dioxide exists as CO_2, so oxygen exists not as O, but as O_2. And nitrogen does not exist in the air as N, but as N_2.

CO_2 and perhaps N_2 came from volcanoes and still come from those that are overflowing with streams of lava from time to time, for lava is full of gas. It may seem strange for gases to come from hot melted rock, but if you take a glass of water and let it stand for some time, you will find that little bubbles of air have collected upon the sides of the glass. That means that the air was in the water and that when the water had been quiet for a time, the air came out and clung to the sides of the glass; that is, the gases you call N_2 and O_2 came from the water and collected in little bubbles that you can see. In this same way, when hot melted rock comes out of the volcanoes, gases of N_2 and CO_2 bubble out and help to increase the air in the world. You know, however, that this air isn't good to breathe, for you must have O_2 in the air in order to live, and so must most of the plants and animals.

Perhaps a little of this O_2 has always been in the air since the hot rocks cooled and let sunlight reach the surface of the earth. However, most of our oxygen comes from that gas CO_2. In the next chapter we will learn how the plants break up the CO_2 and let the gas O_2 go free.

From year to year you may read in books and magazines more about the origin of the air. If those scientists are correct in thinking that the earth very early in its life was a great ball of melted rock, then it is probable that it started even at that early date with a lot of nitrogen in the sky and a small amount of oxygen. Then more gases came from the boiling lava in the volcanoes and formed our air.

3

Seaweed and Jellyfish

Let us now return to those little protists that we left drifting around in the stormy seas of the newly made earth. Slowly, very slowly, they began to grow larger. The larger they grew, the better chance they had to live, for it was hard to live in those troublous times. After a while they could just barely have been seen by the aid of a good microscope. That shows how very, very tiny they were in the beginning.

Some protists were swimmers, and hunted for food and kept away from dangerous places. Soon they developed into different forms, many different kinds; some of the forms into which they developed could be called single-celled animals and plants.

During all this time there was a fierce struggle among protists to keep alive, for there were hot currents in the ocean and cold currents, and waves and ice and steam. Some of the protists grew into little round cells with a little dark center, called a nucleus, like in Figure 3-1. They were and are nearly transparent, as we know because many of their ancient ancestors did.

A very advanced example of a single-celled animal living

today and one which you will probably study in school is the amoeba (Figure 3-1a). You can see how advanced the amoeba is over the single cell, which, if you could see it, looks just like a tiny particle of jelly. Not only can the microscopic amoeba engulf food by means of its false feet but also these "feet" enable it to move around.

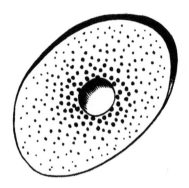

Figures 3-1 and 3-1a.   A simple cell. Notice the nucleus in the center. Compare the cell with the amoeba. How much more complex the amoeba is. But the single cell is a blueprint of the earliest single-celled living things.   *(Bausch & Lomb Optical Co.)*

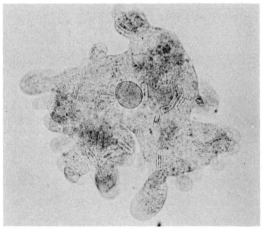

If you are fortunate enough to own a microscope, you can study the amoeba for yourself. You may find some in pond water. During the spring or summer, collect a jar of pond water with some of the plants growing in it. Even if you don't find amoeba, you will probably find other simple animals and plants; many of these will be single-celled.

Perhaps one of the most interesting things that ever happened on this earth was when the little single cells got together in groups and divided the work, so that each cell had its own job to attend to and didn't have to do a little of everything. When you play games, you usually divide the work — some of you guard the goal, while others run with the ball, some pitch the ball, and others spend most of their time catching it. When you divide work like that, you can play many kinds of games. It was the same way with those little groups of cells. As soon as they divided up the work, they found there were many ways of getting food and protecting themselves from danger.

Some of the groups of cells found that they could get their food better by floating about in the water. They didn't think very much about it. They merely kept on floating because the protists from which they had descended had always floated. When they became cells and then when they formed groups of cells, they still kept on floating. Certain cells, however, could do some things better than the others could. Those on the outside could form a surface that protected the cells on the inside. Perhaps those on the inside were busy all the time getting food from the water.

Of course these groups of cells didn't get together and have a meeting and elect someone to act as president. They didn't appoint certain cells to do the eating and others to form a skin or shell and do the protecting, and still others to form fins and tails and do the swimming. Remember that we are talking of a time some 1,000 million years ago (some scientists say some 2,000 million years ago), and single cells just do not do any thinking — worse even than that, they were

and are deaf, dumb, and blind. Yet these groups of cells developed after millions of years into wonderful animals that
could see and hear and talk. They did it very simply by just
experimenting. These experiments were serious, for if they
didn't succeed, the cells usually died, and sometimes the
whole group of cells died. They didn't know that they were
experimenting, for they had no head and no brain. The experimenting was done in the following way:

All groups of cells were not exactly alike. Some were a
little tougher than others, and some could absorb more atoms
of gas from the water than others. When the waves and ocean
currents carried groups of cells against the rocks, those
groups that had a tough outer layer stood a better chance of
surviving. Since children are usually like their fathers and
mothers, the descendants of the little groups of cells with
tough outer layers were usually made in the same way. So
there grew up a number of groups of cells in which the outer
layer was tough. Those groups of cells where by chance the
outer layer happened to be very soft were often damaged and
destroyed. Their descendants inherited the soft outside layer
so that many of them were also killed. And so after a while —
thousands of years — all the groups of this particular kind
would have a tough outer layer, and there would be none with
a soft outside layer. Some of these groups of cells grew together to form perhaps that curious stuff we now call seaweed.

The seaweed grew in the shallow water of the ocean and at
the mouths of rivers. It was seaweed that first gave us most of
the very necessary gas, oxygen, which we have called O_2. For
millions of years the green leaves and grass on the land and
the seaweed in the ocean have given us quantities of oxygen,
so that now one-fifth of the air consists of O_2. How they do it

is more or less of a mystery, but the general method is as follows:

When some groups of cells found they could live by attaching themselves to the rocks, they developed a remarkable ability. Some of the cells that did the eating caught the CO_2 that was dissolved in the water, used the C, and got rid of the O_2. Cells that can behave in this queer way are so complicated that we don't know just how they are made. They are bright green because they have a stuff in them called chlorophyll. The C that the chlorophyll eats is combined with hydrogen and oxygen and finally is built into a substance that makes the stems tough and the trunks and branches of trees hard. It is the chlorophyll that gives the green color to most leaves and to the grass, as well as to nearly all seaweeds.

In the course of millions upon millions of years the seaweeds that lived in shallow water must have become stranded. It was natural, perhaps, that some seaweeds should try to get out of the water and live in the air. They didn't say to their friends, "Let's go and explore the air," just as some of us might say, "Let's go and try to explore Mt. Everest." No one said anything. It took the seaweeds a long time to accomplish it, for they had to have water as well as light in order that their chlorophyll could eat the CO_2. Of course they got plenty of light as soon as they poked their leaves out of the water, and also they found a quantity of CO_2 in the air; but they had to be very careful not to dry up when they were lying in the sun. Perhaps they first got accustomed to the air by lying on the mud flats for a few hours each day when the tide had gone out. Some day you will study astronomy and learn why the tides were probably greater in those days than now. The mud flats at low water were larger than now, so that there was plenty of room for some of the seaweed to get accustomed to the air as it lay in the wet pools on the sand for several hours each day.

After thousands of years a seaweed was developed that had some very clever devices. The cells on the under side of the leaf became elongated. They could absorb moisture and give it to the rest of the leaf. This was the very beginning of roots for plants and trees. The upper cells formed a tough layer to keep the moisture that was inside from getting out. The green chlorophyll was just under this tough layer or skin. You remember, however, that chlorophyll must have light in order to absorb CO_2, keep the atoms of C prisoners, and let the molecules of O_2 go free. Consequently, those leaves that had an outer layer of cells so thick that the light couldn't go through soon died. Only those seaweeds lived that happened to have an upper layer of cells that would let the light through. After a while all the leaves had a thin layer of cells on the outside that would let in light but would not let the leaf dry up.

So far the seaweed had done fairly well. It had got out of its crowded ocean for at least a few hours each day. It had developed an outer layer of cells that let the light through to the chlorophyll and yet kept the moisture inside the leaf. It had developed the cells on the bottom so that they grew long and went into the mud to get moisture for the leaf. There is one thing, however, that we haven't considered, and that is, how did the CO_2 get to the green chlorophyll? Although the outer layer was thin and would let in the light, it wouldn't let any gas like CO_2 get to the green chlorophyll. When the seaweed was in the ocean, it didn't have this trouble, for some of the CO_2 was dissolved in the water, and the seaweed under the water didn't have such a tough outer layer of cells. The seaweed was soaked with water, and the chlorophyll absorbed the CO_2 from the water. On the land, however, the chlorophyll must get the CO_2 from the air or else the plant would die. Probably many plants did die for this very reason.

If some plants by chance had little openings in the tough outer layer of cells, the CO_2 would get through and be absorbed by the green chlorophyll. Plants, like groups of cells and like fishes, are not all just alike. Each individual plant is a little different from its brothers and sisters, just as we are a little different from our brothers and sisters. Perhaps, then, some members of the seaweed families happened to have little holes in this outer layer of tough cells, so that the CO_2 could get through to the chlorophyll. These plants would have a great advantage over their brothers and sisters and cousins. They could stay longer in the air without dying for lack of CO_2. After thousands of years the only plants that were high out of the water on the banks of the rivers down near the seashore were the seaweeds that could let CO_2 get through the little holes in the tough outer layer of cells.

If you had been there, you would have been discouraged as you watched the plants for perhaps a million years trying to live in the air and never succeeding, for when there was a long hot and dry season, the little holes or pores in the leaves let the moisture escape and the plant would dry up and die.

Finally, some plants grew that happened to differ in a very fortunate way from their neighbors. In these plants the outer layer of cells behaved very differently on a dry, sunny day from the way it did on a wet, rainy day. This is rather natural, for even now we don't behave on a hot, sunny day just as we do on a cold, rainy day. On a hot, dry day the outer cells of these peculiar plants crowded together and accidentally closed up those little pores through which the CO_2 got to the chlorophyll. That was rather bad for the plant in one way, for it temporarily prevented the CO_2 from getting inside. This stopping of the pores, however, was also good for the plant, for it kept the moisture from escaping and kept the plant from becoming too dry. As soon, however, as the air became moist — at night or on a rainy day, that is — the cells would separate a little. The little pores then became open once more so that the CO_2 could go through and be absorbed by green chlorophyll. Such plants, in which the outer layer of cells would expand in moist weather and contract in dry, would be able to live much longer away from the water. Since the plants that didn't have this characteristic died, it is plain that all seaweeds that got out of the water and tried to live on the land had these expanding and contracting pores.

In Figure 3-2 you will find a diagram of a plant that is, perhaps, like one of these primitive plants that emerged from the sea. (Some scientists think this happened perhaps about 3,000 million years ago. Remember, this is a very very rough guess — but an educated guess based on much study.) Like so many other things we have read about, there are still plants today that are apparently almost like their primitive ancestors. The diagram shows the way the plant would look if you took a knife and cut through the leaf and then looked at the edge through a microscope. On top you can see that the skin consists of a row of tough single cells. Then you can see a little opening that closes up during a hot, dry day and opens during the moist night or during a rainy day. It must have been a rainy day when this diagram was drawn, for the little pore is open. Underneath the skin you can see the dark green cells that contain the chlorophyll. The CO_2 comes in through this pore and is taken up by the chlorophyll cells. At the bottom of the diagram are the cells that have grown long so that they can get water from the moist earth and pass it along to the other cells and the chlorophyll. Of course, you will remember, the cells are so small they cannot be seen with the naked eye. The pores, too, cannot be seen. The diagram shows the way the plant looks through a microscope.

It is a wonderful device, this, whereby the primitive land plant can keep alive in the air and high up on the bank of the river. We should remember, however, that it took millions of years, and during that time millions of little land plants met with a terrible death, for they dried up and died like travelers lost in a desert. Fortunately, all seaweeds were not alike. Those that had unfortunate shapes died by drying or suffocating. Only those that happened to have good shapes survived.

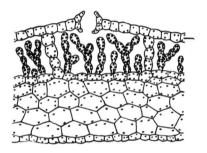

Figure 3-2.   A very early air-living (land) plant might have looked like this if it had been cut by a sharp knife. Notice the opening at the top through which carbon dioxide enters; the cells underneath the upper skin have chlorophyll in them.   (© *General Biological Supply House, Inc., Chicago*)

Even today it is fortunate that we are not all born exactly alike, for if we were all alike, we should all want to do the same thing. As it is, some of us want to be doctors, some try to go to the South Pole, and some teach; so it has been very fortunate that for hundreds of millions of years little seaweeds, little fishes, little monkeys, and little children have not all been exactly alike.

Those groups of cells that clung to the rocks in the water still continued to live very peacefully. They took their food from the gases and mineral matter in the water and lived a quiet and happy life with their neighbors. Sometimes a powerful seaweed would crowd a weaker one just as we have seen a large tree shade the ground from the sun so thoroughly that small trees and plants cannot grow near it; thus, we find a struggle for life even among the plants.

Some of the other groups of cells got food by fastening themselves to the rocks. Then the cells on the outer surface had the job of protecting the other cells from being hurt.

Heretofore these little groups of cells had taken for food the gases that were dissolved in the water. Then others developed in such a way that they began to eat each other for food. Also some of the groups happened to be able to move a little and to push themselves through the water. This gave them a tremendous advantage over those that couldn't, for they could go and get their food instead of waiting for it to float by, and also they could swim away from danger. Perhaps we ought not to call this feeble effort swimming, for they were just barely able to move at first and only went through the water when it was very calm. If there were waves, thousands of these little groups would be killed because they couldn't swim fast enough to get out of the way. You see, therefore, that if one could wiggle his sides fast enough to move out of danger, he had a great advantage. He might live when all his companions were killed. If his children inherited his ability to wiggle, after a long time there would be a whole family of wigglers, which could move away from a storm and could get their food more easily. Finally, such a group of cells grew into a jellyfish. Figure 3-3 is a picture of a jellyfish such as those you can now find in the ocean. We know that they are almost exactly like the jellyfish that lived millions of years ago, for some of those ancient jellyfish got caught in the mud and turned into rock. When these rocks are split open, we sometimes find the imprint of very ancient jellyfish. Plants, fishes, and animals that have been turned into rock after being in the ground for millions of years are called fossils.

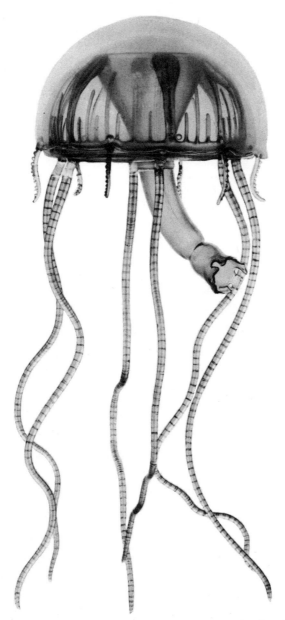

Figure 3-3.   This jellyfish wriggles through our oceans by flapping his sides as did his remote ancestor 500 million years ago. Photograph of an exhibit at the American Museum of Natural History, New York, N. Y.

(American Museum of Natural History)

4

Shells and Fishes

Again we must refer to those cells that are just visible in a microscope. You remember, some of these came together and formed little groups. Some of these groups floated close to the bottom of the shallow water near the shore. They seemed to get better food in this way than they could by attaching themselves to a rock or by floating near the surface. They kept close to the mud and sand where there wasn't much current in the water. To swim fast was no great advantage; however, they did need protection, for there was constant danger that they would be eaten alive by the creatures that could swim. Therefore, if the cells or material on the outside happened to be tough, that group had a very considerable advantage and perhaps wouldn't be eaten by any other marauding group. The offspring of this group would inherit a tough skin. During thousands of years the tough outer skin would actually become hard or, in other animals, a material formed by certain cells in the skin would actually become very hard, like a rock. We now call it a shell, and the little animals that are protected in this way we call shellfish. Some of these shellfish haven't changed very much even down to the present time. In Figure 4-1 you will find two photographs of some shells.

The one on the top is a fossil shell taken from rock that was formed about 500 million years ago. Those on the bottom are living shellfish with animals inside the shells. The animals have stretched their long necks out from the shell probably in search of food. Clams and oysters were developed in this way.

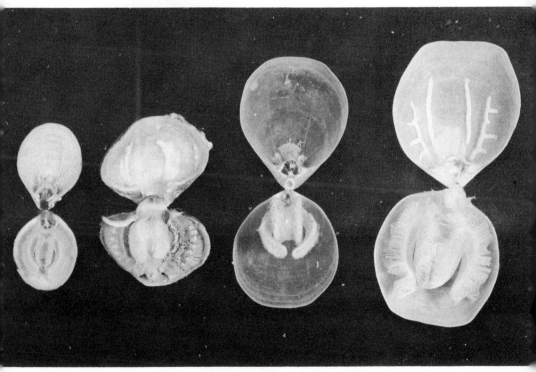

Figure 4-1.   A picture of a fossil lingulella on the top and living successors on the bottom. Very little change in appearance has taken place in millions of years. (Top: *American Museum of Natural History*. Bottom: © *General Biological Supply House, Inc., Chicago*)

Those groups of cells that floated very slowly near the bottom of the shallow parts of the sea didn't all become shellfish. Some developed a tough skin and long arms. They crawled very slowly on the sand and mud. We call some of these animals starfish. These starfish liked to eat the shellfish. It was hard for the starfish to do this unless the shellfish had his head out of his shell while he was hunting for food. Then if the starfish happened to be crawling very slowly over the sand and mud at that time, he would grab the shellfish and eat him.

Once upon a time about 250 million years ago some starfish were attacking and trying to eat some shellfish, just as the starfish now try to eat oysters. But on that day of long ago a heavy mass of mud probably slid down on top of the starfish and shellfish that were fighting in the shallow sea and killed them all. Then the heat in the earth and the great weight of the rocks turned the mud and sand into rock. The starfish and the shellfish had their own material replaced by minerals, so that they turned hard and rocklike. We call animals and plants that have turned this way fossils. Lately the rock was found in New York State and split open, and there were the fossil starfish and shellfish just as they had been millions of years ago when that avalanche of mud prevented the starfish from eating the shellfish. Figure 4-2 is a photograph of that rock.

It seems strange that mud and sand can be turned into rock by merely pressing it and heating it. However, bricks are man-made rock, and they are made by molding clay into the shape of a brick and then heating it for a long time over a hot fire. If you take a handful of mud and squeeze it tight, you know, you can make it into a ball that will keep its shape for some time. Now the earth can squeeze a ball of mud as hard as if one of the wheels of a railroad car were resting on it. It is hot far down in the earth, so that the mud is to some extent

Figure 4-2.   In a place we now call Saugerties, New York, these starfish
were eating shellfish in the far-off Devonian Period just as they eat oysters
today, when they were suddenly covered with mud and later turned into
stone. The shells are plainly visible among the starfish. From *Early Adaptation in the Feeding Habits of Starfishes* by John Mason Clarke, Director
of the New York State Museum, Albany, N. Y.

(N. Y. State Museum and Science Service)

baked. Finally, instead of being squeezed for a few seconds
like your mud ball, the earth keeps this mud baked and
pressed for perhaps millions of years. No wonder mud and
sand under such conditions are turned into rock.

This picture of the starfish shows that the shellfish were
really in great danger. If any shellfish was born with a new

Figure 4-3.   A scene at low tide 500 million years ago. The animals in the long spiral outer shell, related to the squid and octopus, were sometimes fifteen feet long. Notice the trilobite in the lower right-hand corner of the picture. From a mural painting by C. R. Knight.

(© Chicago Natural History Museum)

shape that made it less likely to be eaten, it would have an advantage and not be so apt to meet with a tragic end. While these shellfish probably never changed very much, some new shellfish grew up from little groups of cells that had quite a different shape. The outer layers of the cell, which had to be tough in order to protect the group, developed into a spiral tube. Even today you can pick up shells like these on the beach at the seashore.

While some groups of cells were getting longer and narrower and swimming more rapidly through the water and while others were perishing because they happened to develop a poor shape for swimming, most of the groups stayed as they had been for millions of years. They could move just fast enough and get food enough to stay alive and reproduce. Many of them resemble our jellyfish of today. For some unknown reason there was very little variation among their offspring, so that families of some round jellyfish stayed as round as their grandfathers from generation to generation even to the present time.

However, certain of the descendants of these groups of cells changed a bit and then kept on changing. Some had a tougher outer skin and could swim faster. Apparently through millions of years those that developed a skin were better protected; their children were more likely to live. They swam faster and could get their food more easily, so that fewer of them starved. After a long, long time there grew up a lot of little long-pointed fishes with real skins.

A few of the descendants of these early fishes have changed almost not at all. They are called lancelets (Figure 4-4). Being pointed at each end, they are good swimmers. Perhaps their ancestors were famous among their neighbors

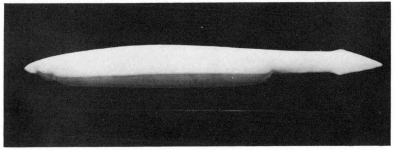

Figure 4-4.   A lancelet. It's about an inch or so long and is of interest as an early type with a notocord, which led to animals with backbones.

(American Museum of Natural History)

because for the first time in the world a skin had been developed behind which the owner could have some privacy. Later, much, much later, the fishlike animals were to develop even a tougher skin with scales. But the really important thing these lancelets had that separated them once and for all from the earlier animals was a tough rod, called a notocord, which braced them up on the inside. The notocord acts very much like your backbone; in fact, our own backbones start with a notocord.

5

Mountains and Rivers

We have been talking about the sea, but we haven't said a word about land and rivers and how these things came to exist. Why should some land project above the ocean and why should there be such a thing as a river? We want to know why some of the land is so steep and high that we call it a mountain. We must for a while leave our little protists and our fishes, and even our oxygen and nitrogen, and try to find out why the land rises above the waters and why the rivers flow into the ocean and why mountains rise up so high that their tops are covered with snow.

You remember that there were huge shooting stars falling on the earth and making it larger. Finally there were no more large stars left to fall, so the earth stopped growing. You remember also that these huge stars struck the earth with such tremendous force that the rock was melted. In this way the earth got a severe pounding. It was kneaded in much the way dough is kneaded when you make bread. Some parts of the earth are very heavy, for they are made of what we call lead and iron and other metals. Also some parts of the earth are lighter than iron, as, for example, ordinary rock. In the course of time — millions of years — as the earth got well pounded and kneaded, many of the light parts like ordinary rock got forced to the surface and most of the heavy parts like iron sank down toward the center, or so we think.

When the shooting stars stopped falling and the surface of the earth began to cool, some of these lighter parts that we call common rock made islands in the hot and forming crust. Perhaps after a while all these islands came together and formed one big piece that we call a continent. A German scientist thinks that they acted in this way, and some of the English and American scientists agree with him. You know bubbles on the water sometimes gather into one large cluster. In a way somewhat similar, these islands of rock came together and formed one large continent. It was a very large continent, for it was North and South America, Europe, Africa, Asia, and Australia all in one. For reasons we don't really know much about, this huge mass of land later separated into several pieces. Australia went off by itself and became a huge island in the South Pacific Ocean. Then South America began to separate from Africa just as if it were a map that was being torn. This separation took tens of millions of years until finally North America, which was the last continent to draw away, had quite separated from Europe. Then for millions of years North and South America slowly, very slowly, slid toward the setting sun, until now the broad Atlantic Ocean lies between them and Europe. If you look at a map of the world and imagine North and South America pushed up against Europe and Africa, you will see that the two great masses of land would fit together very nicely. No one really knows whether this did happen or not, so some of the scientists of the leading nations of the world are measuring the distances from one continent to another just as carefully as they possibly can and hope in a few years to find out whether or not the continents are still moving apart.

You remember that when we began this story, we found that the earth was so hot that all the water in the ocean was turned into steam and rose up in the sky in the form of dense clouds. Then torrents of rain fell down and even before they reached the earth were turned again into steam. Finally the earth cooled enough to form a crust, and when that got cold and hard, the rain could stay on the earth without boiling and becoming steam. Then oceans grew in the hollow places, and there was blue sky with only occasional storms.

The rain on these great continents that we have been describing settled into the hollow places and formed big pools of water, which we now call ponds and lakes. After a while so much water poured into these lakes that they overflowed. The overflowing water then wore a channel all the way to the ocean. These channels we call rivers.

A river is constantly wearing away the land and carrying earth from its bottom and sides down to the ocean. You know how the rain during a thunderstorm cuts deep ruts into soft ground that is not held firmly by grass, and you know how muddy the water is that flows off such ground. These little streams made by a thundershower behave just like rivers. They wear away the ground and carry it downstream. Sometimes a stream will flow into a pool of water. Then all the earth the stream is carrying is deposited in the pool of water close to where the stream entered. After a while the deposit is so big that it sticks out from the water and forms new land. In geography we call land made in this way a delta (Figure 5-1).

If a thunderstorm lasted all summer, you know that all the dirt that wasn't held firmly by grass, by roots of trees, and by rocks would be washed away and deposited far off where the brooks flow into some larger pond or where the rivers flow into the ocean.

This wearing away of the higher land and the forming of

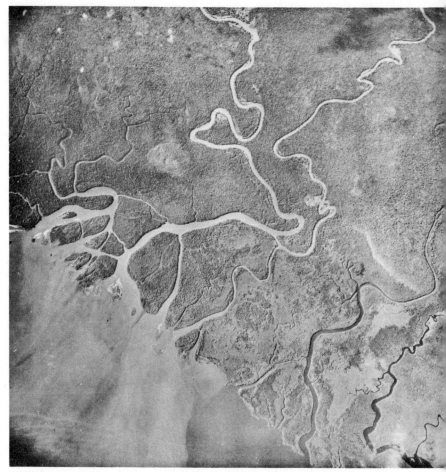

Figure 5-1. Do you see the land added to the mainland by the soil carried by rivers? This delta was deposited in the Netherlands East Indies.

(U.S. Department of the Air Force)

new land at the edge of the ocean is going on all the time, even if we don't have thundershowers all summer long, for the water is always carrying little particles of soil from the high land to the low land and eventually to the seashore.

You may think that after a while all the soil would be washed away and only rock would be left and then there would be nothing more to be deposited at the seashore. That would be true if it weren't that the rock that is exposed to the air is always slowly turning into small particles of soil. The next time you see a place where a road has been cut through a hill of solid rock, you will probably see that the rock at the bottom of this cut near the road is solid and not cracked, while the rock near the top of the cut is cracked and sometimes merges into the soil so gradually that you can hardly tell where the soil begins and the rock leaves off. The picture, Figure 5-2, shows how soil is formed in this way. This is partly due to our old friends O_2 and CO_2. These gases, dissolved in water, attack the rock and over the years make it crumble just like dead wood. Then the rain comes and washes these

Figure 5-2.   This cut in the earth shows what is going on underneath the trees and bushes. By the action of water and air the rock crumbles and becomes soil.   *(U.S. Forest Service)*

newly formed particles of dirt down into the valleys, and the rivers carry some of it to the seashore.

While all this is going on, another great thing is happening: the earth is continuing to cool, and as it cools, it grows a little smaller. Perhaps, also, it is growing smaller, very slowly, because deep down near the center of the earth the atoms and molecules that make up the rock are getting closer and closer together. The crust of rock on which the oceans rest and on which the great island continents of light rock rest cannot get much smaller than it now is, for it has already nearly cooled off. Consequently, this crust of the earth is bound to wrinkle (Figure 5-3). It wrinkles for about the same reason

Figure 5-3.   Southeast of Atoka, Oklahoma, is this excellent sample of the wrinkling and folding of the earth's crust.   *(Standard Oil Co., N.J.)*

that a dried apple wrinkles. These wrinkles usually come at the weakest places, for at such places the bending of the skin or crust is easiest.

The weakest places in the crust of the earth were sometimes near the seashore and sometimes where mud had been deposited at the bottom of inland seas for millions of years.

Since the inland seas and the shores are weak places, the crust of the earth began to fold at these points, and these folds we call mountains. In the course of millions of years huge mountains rose where once there had been only water. Figure 5-3 is a picture of some wrinkles in the layers of rock. Figure 5-4 is a model of the way some of these wrinkles in the crust

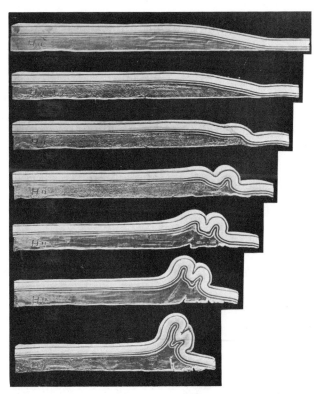

Figure 5-4.   How folds in the earth's crust are made. Models of experiments imitate the folds found in mountain ranges.   *(U.S. Geological Survey)*

of the earth would look if you were a giant and could cut a slice right out of the earth.

During all this time there were frequent storms, as there are now. Rain fell on the mountains and drained off into little brooks and then into rivers and finally into the ocean. Just as before, the water carried off every loose particle of sand and soil that it could get hold of. Gradually through millions of years these mountains were worn down, smoothed over, and thus made much lower and smaller. Then instead of mountain torrents plunging in a series of cascades down steep slopes into the valleys, there were sluggish streams, which very slowly flowed down low hills, or through long plains into the ocean (Figure 5-5).

But still mud and sand were deposited, layer after layer, along the edges of the great land masses and sank by their own weight deep down into the crust of the earth, where they were baked and pressed into rock. Always the earth kept on growing a little smaller. Always the crust, which couldn't grow any smaller, had to fold and wrinkle in its weakest places, and these places were usually where the layers of mud and sand had sunk deep down into the earth.

Probably we ought not to say that the making of mountains has been always going on. Although the earth was continually cooling, there would be times when it hadn't shrunk enough to make the crust wrinkle. Then again there would be other times when the crust would wrinkle a great deal and would catch up with the slowly shrinking earth. So there have been formed successive mountain ranges. Sometimes new wrinkles will form in the very places where old wrinkles have been worn away. Once upon a time, where Massachusetts and Connecticut now are, great wrinkles were formed. After millions of years these mountains were all worn away by rain and snow. Then a new wrinkle came, the land rose several hun-

Figure 5-5.   The Connecticut River winds its way through the farm lands between Northhampton and Springfield. The river seems to wander back and forth; this is called meandering.   *(Standard Oil Co., N.J.)*

dred feet, and once more the rivers started on their long, tedious wearing away of the land and carrying the soil particles down to the seashore. They are still patiently doing it. The Connecticut River has cut out for itself a broad valley so that you would hardly believe, as you cross it now, that it once rushed into Long Island Sound between high cliffs, which it had cut from the rock. Of course this land did not rise in a few days or in a few centuries. It possibly took thousands of years to rise, but even so, it rose faster than the river could wear it away.

The way a stream cuts first a deep canyon and then a broad valley is very interesting. As we said before, when a stream after a thundershower is cutting its way through soft ground, it makes a little canyon, for the channel is narrow and the sides almost perpendicular. To an insect it would be a deep chasm through the bottom of which a mountain torrent was rushing. If you watch this stream for a few minutes, you will find that it is cutting away the dirt from the bottom of the insect's cliffs. This is called undermining the sides of the cliffs. Soon large sections of the sides begin to fall into the stream. It is possible to watch such a little rivulet make a wider and wider valley through the soft ground. Mountain rivers behave in just this way. While a little stream caused by a thundershower cuts a wide canyon in a few minutes through the soft earth, a mountain river will take thousands of years to cut a broad canyon through solid rock (Figure 5-6).

When the canyon becomes broad and the sides merely smooth sloping hills, the wearing away of the rock and the further widening of the valley becomes more difficult, for the stream now moves more slowly because it has worn away the high land that had made it a torrent. It has widened its valley until it flows through a level plain of considerable extent. Then the river wanders over this plain, but every now and then it will wear a channel close to the side of the valley. In this way it digs a little more from the sides of the hills, and so gradually, very slowly, the valley is widened. This wandering of the river is called meandering (Figure 5-5).

The sharp curves in the stream are constantly changing their positions, for the water eats away the bank on the outer edge and deposits earth on the inner edge. These sharp curves slowly travel down the valley. As they move, they are always carrying away part of the higher land on each side of the

Figure 5-6. This river has cut a deep channel, but it has not had time to make a broad valley. Grand Canyon of the Yellowstone River, Yellowstone National Park.   *(Union Pacific Railroad Photo)*

broad valley. In thousands and sometimes millions of years the brooks, the mountain torrents, and the meandering streams will carry away all the mountains and hills and leave the country almost a level plain, which is called a peneplain, because "pene" in Latin means "almost."

Mountains that are old have been worn into smooth shapes and are not so very high. As a rule, they have very few precipices or deep gorges and canyons, for all these rough edges have been worn away. On the other hand, newly formed wrinkles or mountains are usually very high and full of sharp peaks and steep sides and deep canyons through which, sometimes, mountain torrents are rushing. The new mountains are just like the soft ground after a thunderstorm. They are full of

Figure 5-7.   Rain and snow — and air — are wearing (eroding) this mountain down.   *(National Park Service)*

sharp edges and cliffs. After millions of years the river in the canyon cuts out a broad valley, and the sharp peaks of the mountains are worn into rounded hills.

The Appalachian Mountains are very old and have become well rounded and covered with bushes and trees. The Rocky Mountains, on the other hand, are a much newer range. Figure 5-7 gives some idea of the way they are being cut away by wind and rain.

How are some mountains worn away? Thin slabs of rock, loosened by rain, which dissolves some of the gases in the air, are broken away from the cliff because the rock expands in the hot sunlight and contracts when it is cold at night. Nearly everything grows a little larger when it is hot and shrinks a

Figure 5-8.   Slowly, very slowly, the domes of these mountains are eroding away; bit by bit over thousands of years, air, snow, and rain crumble the solid rock.   *(Santa Fe Railway)*

little when it is cold, and these great ledges of rock are no exception. Even though this movement of rock is very, very small, it is enough to break off large slabs. Stone Mountain, near Atlanta, Georgia, has been rounded off in this manner.

6

Volcanoes

Sometimes as the crust of the earth has wrinkled and jammed by the slow cooling and shrinking of the earth, cracks have been made in the rocks, and then the hot melted rock from far down in the earth has come out and flowed over the land like molasses. We call melted rock that bubbles up from inside the earth *lava*. Sometimes the crack in the earth is shaped more or less like a round hole, and when the lava comes out, it spreads all around that hole and cools into rock. Sometime later more lava comes and flows over the mound and makes it higher. After a long, long time the mound grows into a mountain, which we call a volcano. The hole in the center through which the hot melted lava occasionally comes is called the crater. Sometimes the lava is actually hot enough to boil in the crater, and then great masses of gas, steam, and smoke come out from the top of the volcano. Figure 6-1 is a picture of a volcano. Occasionally melted rock, or lava as we call it, not only flows down the side of a mountain but keeps on flowing over the land below and burying everything that is in its path.

When a city is near a volcano, it is always in danger of being buried some day by a great mass of lava that may flow

Figure 6-1.   Mt. Vesuvius, Italy, erupting. Why don't plants grow on the volcano's side and base?   *(Fotoagenzia Napoli)*

down the sides of the mountain. Nearly two thousand years ago there was a city in Italy named Pompeii, which got buried in this way. Many Romans lived in this city, and many of them were killed when the city was buried. During the last hundred years the Italians have dug away the ashes and lava and dirt that covered Pompeii so that now we can study the ruins of houses two thousand years old and can understand how people lived in that long-ago time. Figure 6-2 is a picture of the ruins as they are today; it also shows how the city

Figure 6-2.   Pompeii, buried by an eruption of Vesuvius, now dug up and restored as you see it here. When you go to Naples, be sure to visit it.
(Alinari Fratelli)

looked when the Romans lived there. Even a volcanic eruption is very useful sometimes, for, you see, it can tell us by burying and so preserving a city how people lived long ago. It was unfortunate for the Romans who got caught in the streets of Pompeii and were killed, but tens of thousands of people have been killed by volcanoes in many parts of the world in all ages since man has been on this earth.

There is a great park out in the Rocky Mountains called the Yellowstone National Park. The Yellowstone River has been flowing through this part of the country for millions of years, so that it has had time to wear away a deep channel (Figure 5-6). The sides of this channel are still deep, for even in thousands of years it hasn't had time to wear away the sides and carry their mud and sand to the ocean. These cliffs on the banks of the river show what happened in this part of the continent millions of years ago, for near the bottom of the cliff you will find buried the stumps of huge trees that have been turned into stone (Figure 6-3). They are called petrified trees or petrified wood. A long time ago there was a great forest

Figure 6-3.   Millions of years ago this fossil tree was part of a luxuriant forest. Under it lie fourteen buried forests. Once more and perhaps for the last time, the great volcanoes that surrounded what is now Yellowstone National Park threw out masses of ashes and pumice stone, and the last, the fourteenth, forest was buried. Now the rain and the Yellowstone River have worn away the ashes that have been turned into rock, and this tree trunk, now a fossil, once more stands erect in the sunlight.

(National Park Service)

where these petrified stumps are now buried. Then there was a volcanic eruption of ashes, which covered the forest and eventually helped turn the stumps of the trees to stone.

After a very long time the rain and the action of oxygen in the air turned some of these ashes into little particles of soil. Then seeds blew in and sprouted. Finally a whole new forest grew on top of that layer of old petrified stumps.

But the most remarkable thing about that cliff on the banks of the Yellowstone River is that, as you climb up from the bottom, you will find fourteen layers of these petrified forests (Figure 6-4). Fourteen times a great forest had grown

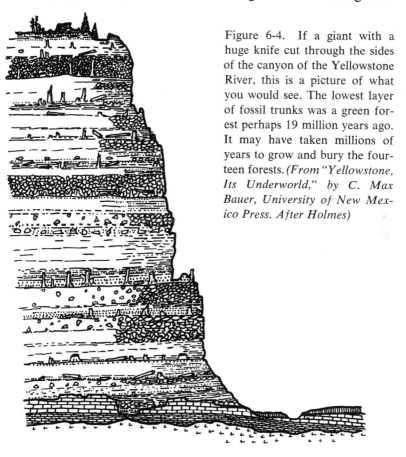

Figure 6-4. If a giant with a huge knife cut through the sides of the canyon of the Yellowstone River, this is a picture of what you would see. The lowest layer of fossil trunks was a green forest perhaps 19 million years ago. It may have taken millions of years to grow and bury the fourteen forests. *(From "Yellowstone, Its Underworld," by C. Max Bauer, University of New Mexico Press. After Holmes)*

in this spot, and fourteen times it had been overwhelmed by ashes from volcanic outbursts. Think how long it must have taken for each forest to grow! Fourteen times that catastrophe happened, and fourteen times ages were used in making a new forest. This is another example both of the tremendous age of the earth and also of how much we can learn from buried cities, forests, and fossils.

7

The Silurian Period

The time when the little protists developed into many-celled animals was so long ago that we might say it was at the very dawn of the history of life on this earth. For hundreds of millions of years changes in sea-dwelling animal life and seaweeds took place very slowly. It would hardly have been necessary to have a calendar in those days, for one year followed another in a monotonous and endless succession. However, when the sea became crowded and the plants and animals began to explore the land, some queer things happened, and the history of the earth became more exciting. From this time on we will give a name to each great period of time.

You know how we measure our own history in years; that is, we say we are ten or fifteen years old. The history of America is so long that we sometimes give a name to a whole group of years; we speak, for example, of the Colonial Period, which was more than a hundred years long. Also we read about the times of the Greeks or the Romans, and each one of these periods was several hundred years long. The Egyptian Period lasted for several thousand years. Therefore, when we want to describe a long time, we are accustomed to give a name to a group of years. In the same way, the history of the earth has been divided into periods, but the time of each of these periods is enormously long —so long that the Egyptian Period seems but a moment in comparison. To some extent we are prepared for long periods in the history of the earth, for you remember those fourteen fossil forests in the Yellowstone National Park and the ages it must have taken to grow a forest of huge trees fourteen times in succession. Therefore, you will not be surprised to learn that the periods in the earth's history are always measured in millions of years.

The period when the land probably began to be covered with plants and when the fishes, the supposed first air-breathing animals, came out of the water to live on land is called the Silurian Period. We think it began 360 million years ago and lasted about 35 million years.

All forms of life are described by two names, "flora" and "fauna." Trees, plants, seaweed, and grass are called flora, and fauna is the name for all other kinds of life such as fishes, clams, insects, birds, and human beings. The flora were the first forms of life to explore and to learn how to live on the land (Figure 7-1). In this Silurian Period some of the fauna were crowded out of the water and tried living for at least a part of the time on the land. Scorpions were probably the pioneers. They were not our ancestors, however, for having become scorpions and having learned to live on the land, they were apparently satisfied with themselves, for they have stayed scorpions ever since. They, therefore, among the fauna, have the longest family tree of air-breathing ancestors.

Apparently the scorpions and their relatives are descended from a jointed sea worm with thick tough skin such as beetles now have. These worms may in their turn have descended from something very much like an elongated jellyfish, which happened to develop into a tough-skinned, slow-moving worm.

Figure 7-1.   The shores of North America in the Silurian Period. The Silurian seaweed is lying in the sun on masses of coral. From a painting by Charles R. Knight.   (© *Chicago Natural History Museum*)

This worm developed a pair of legs for each of several joints in its body, and then after millions of years one of its descendants developed into a scorpion (Figure 7-2), continuing to live under water until the Silurian, when it came up on land and became an air-breather. Some of its relatives, however, continued to live in the sea. Because of their appearance, these animals are known as "sea scorpions." The sea scorpions seem to have been very efficient both in defending themselves and in getting food, and soon became enormous

Figure 7-2. Models of the enormous sea scorpions as they might have been in the Silurian sea. How many do you find?

(© *Chicago Natural History Museum*)

creatures; some fossil sea scorpions of this period that were three feet long have been found in New York State. Figure 7-3 is a picture of one of these monsters.

Some of the small sea scorpions probably had a hard time to get enough food and at the same time not be killed and eaten by the big scorpions. Meanwhile, the earth's crust wrinkled more and more and the seas kept drying up — slowly — very slowly.

In adapting themselves to air and sunlight, the scorpions must have suffered as many tragic experiences as the plants. Millions of scorpions probably perished before a type appeared that didn't have to go back to the ocean at high water in order to keep from drying up and dying. Fortunately for

Figure 7-3.   The fossil remains of this crustacean were found near Buffalo, New York. His name is Stylonurus and he was three feet long. From an exhibit in the New York State Museum, Albany, New York.

(N.Y. State Museum and Science Service)

us, land scorpions were small in comparison with some of their cousins in the sea, and they have remained small even to the present time (Figure 7-4). Figure 7-5 is a picture of one of these scorpions that became a fossil. Some of these were two and a half inches long.

Figure 7-4. This is a picture of one of our own living scorpions. He lives by eating insects and hunts by night. The sting is at the end of the tail.
(U.S. Department of Agriculture Photograph)

Millions of years after the scorpions came out of the sea, other land forms crawled from the mud flats and climbed over the rocks. They, too, scientists think, were descended from those same sea worms that were the ancestors of the scorpions. They haven't changed much in the several hundred million years during which they have been living on dry land.

The plants of the Silurian Period were very simple and much like that seaweed that first tried to live on land. These plants were less than a foot high. Their roots were very weak and were used mostly for drawing water from the ground — not, as roots are today, for holding the plant erect as well as for drawing water.

In any event, life has come out of the ocean, and some plants, scorpions, and millipeds are living on the land, and the seas are beginning to dry out. Many of them are quite

Figure 7-5.   A fossil scorpion in the rocks of the Silurian Period. Compare this with Figure 7-3. Do you see how scientists can build a model such as in Figure 7-3 from the fossil such as the one above?

(American Museum of Natural History)

shallow. Sometimes the seas were so shallow that they would evaporate in hot sunlight and leave only dry land. Of course any salt that was in the water was left on the land.

When water disappears into the air in this way, it is said to evaporate. You can illustrate this by filling a dish with salt water and letting it stand for a few days. It will evaporate, and you will find all the salt that you had dissolved in the water left on the dish in the form of a very thin coating. If, without removing the salt, you fill the dish again and again with salt water and each time allow the water to evaporate, you will find that the coating of salt in the dish grows deeper and deeper. If you keep evaporating the salt water for a long enough time, you will have a thick layer of salt in the dish.

Some of these shallow seas behaved just like a dish of salt water. For millions of years they were alternately dry land and then shallow sea, until the layer of salt at the bottom became sometimes several hundred feet thick. During the Silurian Period such a sea existed over a large part of the state of New York. After the salt had been spread over hundreds of square miles, it was covered with sand and mud. Now these beds of salt are mined and provide you with most of the salt that you eat.

Such a bed of salt may some day be formed near Salt Lake City in the state of Utah. You have probably heard how very salty the water is in the Great Salt Lake, which was, many thousands of years ago, much larger than it is today. It has gradually dried up until now only a small and shallow lake is left. If this lake should dry up completely, it would leave a thick layer of salt.

You remember that in the beginning, the waters were not as salty as they are now. When this lake in Utah was large and covered part of the states of Nevada, Colorado, and Utah, its water might be called "fresh." We say water is fresh when it is good to drink; however, even such water contains just a trace of salt, but so little that you cannot taste it. All the springs, brooks, and rivers dissolve out of the rocks and soil some of the little particles that we call salt. The salts are carried into the ocean, and there they stay forever. This is because the ocean behaves like the salt water in that dish. When the sun evaporates the water of the ocean and forms clouds, the salt is left behind. Then the rain falls from the clouds and soaks into the land and forms springs, which dissolve from the ground more of the salts. The sea, therefore, acts like a huge mousetrap. It catches all the little particles of salt and lets none escape. You are probably thinking that the ocean is growing more salty all the time, and that is exactly the truth. It is growing more salty so slowly, however, that even Columbus, if he came back to the earth, would notice no difference.

This lake that thousands of years ago covered so much of the state of Utah has been named Lake Bonneville. It behaved in a small way just like the ocean. All the brooks and rivers that flowed into Lake Bonneville carried tiny particles of salt. When the sun, however, evaporated the water and formed clouds, the salt was left in the lake. Finally a dry period came and the water evaporated much faster than it could be supplied by the streams. Now a much smaller and very salty lake is left, which we call Great Salt Lake. Figure 7-6 is a picture of the old beaches that were made by the waves of Lake Bonneville. Now of course they are high and dry on the sides of the hills.

If the water in a lake can flow into the ocean, the lake remains fresh and good to drink, because the water in it is then being constantly changed. The old water flows out, and new water from the streams takes its place. Although this water contains a few particles of salt, we cannot taste them, and so we call the water fresh.

It is very different when the country is dry and hot, so that the water in a lake is evaporated as fast as new water can

flow into it from streams and rivers. Then the little particles
of salt cannot flow away to the ocean. They are caught in the
trap and cannot escape. Each day more and more are brought
to the lake by streams and brooks until after thousands of

Figure 7-6.   Picture a large lake lapping on the "beaches" that are now on
the side of the hill. Lake Bonneville's waters once lapped on these beaches.
(U.S. Geological Survey)

years the lake becomes so full of little particles of salt that it
is not good to drink and we call it a salt lake (Figure 7-7).
Then if a dry period comes and the streams stop flowing, the
lake gradually becomes dry and the great accumulation of
salt particles is left as a white crust on the land.

Sometimes dust and sand are blown over this layer of salt,
and sometimes the basin where the lake used to be is again

filled with water — perhaps a part of an inland sea. Mud is then deposited on top of the sand and dust until finally the layer of salt is buried deep in the earth. If this sea later disappears, we can dig into these great beds and cut out tons of

Figure 7-7.   You are looking at Great Salt Lake. The Wasatch Mountains are in the background.   *(Union Pacific Railroad Photo)*

rock salt, which we grind into the fine white powder that we use in our food. A salt mine used by the ancient Indians of America about two thousand years ago was discovered in Nevada. When the mine was discovered, many of the tools used by the ancient Indians were found. Explorers even found partly eaten ears of ancient corn that perhaps had been taken into the mine for a noonday lunch.

8

The Devonian Period

The next period is called Devonian. It began about 325 million years ago when the Silurian Period ended, and lasted about 45 million years. It is a very important period in our family history, for it was during this 45 million years that some animals that later became our ancestors came out of the fresh water and started their long career on the land. They are called amphibians, for they lived part of the time in the water and part of the time on land. Frogs of today are also amphibians. Like many other animals who lived ages ago, this amphibian ancestor made himself known by leaving his fossil. The old fellow may have looked much like the picture in Figure 8-1. Because some of the fossils of later generations have been found in rocks, and for various other reasons, it has been possible to draw a picture that gives some idea of the way this early ancestor appeared. The name given to him was Eusthenopteron.

The shallow water held a great danger for fishes — the danger of being stranded at ebb tide. Surely many fishes must have suffocated on those occasions, for they couldn't breathe without water. Their fins made very poor legs with which to crawl back into the ocean. You can see what a great advantage a fish would have if he could breathe air and have fins to help him crawl toward other bodies of water (Figure 8-1). He would be much more apt to survive. Since fishes are not all just alike, some, called riphidistians, could indeed breathe air and crawl over the land with lobe-shaped fleshy fins. Their children inherited fins of this shape. Also the fins of the children were not all just alike. Those fish-children that happened to have fins more suitable for crawling had a still better chance to escape drying and dying on the flats at low tide. Also, it may be that the continents rose a little as the shrinking earth made the crust squirm and heave. Then the inland seas, perhaps, became shallow until only mud flats and small pools remained. The fish caught in this manner must breathe air part of the time or die. Of course these changes took millions of years. So gradually a fish's fin became a foot.

Figure 8-1.   This mud skipper now found in tropical mangrove swamps perhaps illustrates crudely (but of course not accurately) the way in which our ancestors changed a fin into a foot. He flops over the mud flats with considerable speed, but he has never developed feet as our amphibian ancestors did.   *(American Museum of Natural History)*

The way a fin might have developed over the ages is illustrated in Figure 8-2. The fin became a flapper or a paddle,

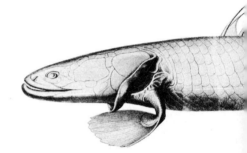

Figure 8-2.   Below is a fringe-fin (like the lobe-fin in Figure 8-2a) on a fish. Above is the kind of foot in an early amphibian into which it may have developed. *(American Museum of Natural History)*

and then the paddle became a foot. At first the fin was merely a tough fold in the fish's skin. As the skeleton developed, the fin developed fine bones. You can see these bones in Figure 8-2a. In b, the bones became larger. Finally in c, the "foot stage," five toes were developed. This is the origin of our

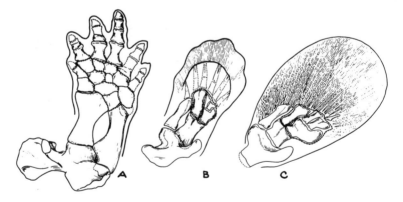

Figure 8-2a.   From lobe-fin (or paddle) to foot. At the left (a) you see the lobe-fin of a kind of fish that may have been a type leading to the development of a land-type foot. The middle smaller lobe-fin (b) is a possible development into (c) an early amphibian foot.

(American Museum of Natural History)

five toes on each foot or five fingers on each hand. It was only a few million years ago that we first stood erect and used our forelegs as "arms" with five fingers at the end of each arm. During nearly all the 300 million years since our ancestor the amphibian developed a foot, our family has moved around on four feet, and each foot has had the five toes that ancestral

Figure 8-3. Cheirolepis, a primitive fish that abounded in Devonian waters.
(American Museum of Natural History)

amphibian found so convenient when he wished to get back into the water. Perhaps there was a period when our amphibian ancestors had one big toe and two rather clumsy smaller toes on each foot, and then they later developed the familiar five toes.

Life on the bottom of the ocean, where the water wasn't too deep, had become very interesting during this period. Many sponges and corals had developed. Some of these became fossils and have been found near Olean in the state of New York. They are now reproduced in the New York State Museum at Albany. Figure 8-4 is a picture of this exhibit. The seaweeds grew tall and had fantastic shapes. Also the shellfish in some cases became so strong that they could catch and

Figure 8-4. Sponges and seaweed from the shallow Devonian seas, which once covered Cattaraugus County, New York. From a photograph of an exhibit at the New York State Museum at Albany.

(*N.Y. State Museum and Science Service*)

eat small, slow-moving fish. These little sluggish fish were protected somewhat by their thick, bony armor. However, this means of protection was only partially successful, as you can see by looking at the picture in Figure 8-5, where a large shellfish is shown eating a small armored fish. Some of these small, slow-moving fish would have perished entirely and become extinct if it had not been for their very large families. More were born than could possibly be killed by their enemies, and so they kept their family name in the ocean for many generations.

If there had been social life among the early dwellers of the sea, trilobite would have been a very common name. From early pre-Silurian times the trilobites had crawled over the bottom of the shallow seas. Finally, it is thought, their enemies became too powerful, and they ceased to exist. The small crustacean that is being eaten alive by a large shellfish

Figure 8-5.   A Devonian shellfish eating a small armored crustacean, a trilobite.   *(N.Y. State Museum and Science Service)*

in Figure 8-5 is a trilobite. Figure 8-6 shows the way a trilobite looked, for many of them have been found fossilized in the rocks. But in the Devonian, the trilobites were on their way to extinction.

Figure 8-6.   How many fossil trilobites do you find pressed into this rock?
(American Museum of Natural History)

It is hard to tell why this ancient and large family met with so hard a fate. That they were very old-fashioned and didn't change their way of living to suit new conditions couldn't have been the reason, because we find horseshoe crabs that are very much like those of today (Figure 8-7). If a horseshoe crab could survive, you would think that a trilobite could, but the fact is that he did not.

Bothriolepis (Figure 8-8), on the other hand, did not survive — although this fish was armored. Bothriolepis was a first cousin of Dinichthys, a savage fish with an enormous mouth. It was in the latter part of the Devonian Period that a group of Bothriolepis in Canada were swimming upstream one day in search of food when they were suddenly buried by a landslide of mud. It overwhelmed them so quickly that they couldn't even move. Then more mud covered them until they were so deep down in the earth that they were finally baked and pressed into rock. Millions of years afterward, the earth

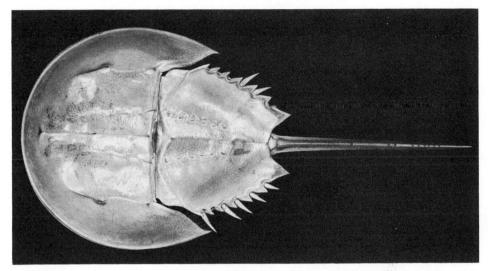

Figure 8-7. A horseshoe crab is a survivor of one of the oldest kinds of animals. Horseshoe crabs trace their ancestry to animals very similar to this one who lived over half a billion years ago.

(American Museum of Natural History)

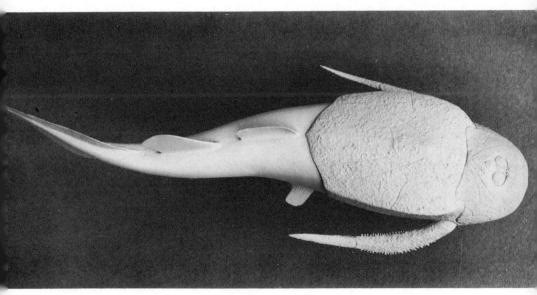

Figure 8-8. A close view of a model of a late Devonian armored fish — Bothriolepis. Can you see why they were heavily protected?

(American Museum of Natural History)

wrinkled at this place and the rock containing these fossils was raised. Then rain and streams wore away enough of the rock to uncover them. Finally a scientist found them there and placed them in a museum.

Some armored fishes grew to a great size. They were successful in getting food. Yet they, too, at last became extinct. As yet we do not know how this happened. Figure 8-9 is a picture of the armored fishes in the Devonian Period.

Figure 8-9.   A scene in the late Devonian in northern Scotland. Can you find a Bothriolepis?   *(American Museum of Natural History)*

You will recall that in the Silurian Period the plants were small, with rootlike structures. Now in the Devonian Period the roots had undergone a different development and had grown stronger, and the plants grew so large as to look like trees, sometimes forty feet high. They are called tree ferns. These tree ferns made the first great forests that spread over the earth. Compared with those of today, they were queer-looking trees, as you can see from the pictures in Figures 8-10 and 8-11. A large forest of these tree ferns grew at Gilboa, New York. Many fossil trunks, branches, and leaves have been found and are now in the New York State Museum at Albany.

You have probably seen a common weed called a horsetail. It is one of the most ancient plants that we have. It appeared in the Devonian Period and then in the next period developed into a very large plant, which looked like a tree, but it couldn't maintain so distinguished a position in the plant world. The big ones died, and now after millions of years, only humble

Figure 8-10.   A forty-foot tree in the silent Devonian forest, for the scorpions and centipedes never spoke and amphibians were not among our noisy ancestors.   *(N.Y. State Museum and Science Service)*

Figure 8-11.   A Devonian forest. Do you see giant tree ferns and club mosses?
(© *Chicago Natural History Museum*)

weeds have survived. We must always remember, however, that it had illustrious uncles in the ancient plant world.

Club mosses have the same family history as horsetails. They are very common, and probably you have often seen them. They had begun to grow tall in the Devonian Period, and then after becoming as huge as trees, the large ones perished and only the small ones survived. Ferns, too, are well-known plants that appeared in the world at this time.

The scorpions and millipeds that came from the water in the last period were now well adapted to breathing air. A

primitive winged insect probably flitted around among the
trees of the Devonian forests for the first time in the history
of the earth. Then there appeared a first spider.

The North America of the Silurian Period showed a Gulf
of Mexico extending in a long narrow sea north to the Gulf
of St. Lawrence. Such a sea is a weak place in the crust of
the earth. In this period the place that yielded as the crust of
the earth crumpled and folded was the part of the country
now called New England, Nova Scotia, and New Brunswick.
This folding made great mountains, which covered the land
and extended far out into what is now the sea, rising high in

the air over the Newfoundland Banks, where today so many of our fish are caught.

South Carolina, North Carolina, and Virginia were also covered with mountains at this time. These folds and wrinkles caused the crust to crack so that masses of molten rock came to the surface. Sometimes this molten rock was very hard after it had cooled. In many cases the rock that we call granite is all that is left of the once majestic mountains that rose to the clouds. The White Mountains of New Hampshire are perhaps the granite cores of larger peaks that covered New England.

Near the place that is now Montreal in Canada a small crack was made in the crust of the earth, and lava and hot gases were thrown out like water from a fountain. The lava cooled after it had flowed a short distance, and so in the course of time it formed a mountain, which, as you know, we call a volcano. This particular volcano is now named Mt. Royal. But it has been millions of years since Mt. Royal spouted lava from its crater, and now in winter it makes a wonderful toboggan slide.

Although along the Atlantic Coast folds in the land caused mountains and volcanoes and made it very dangerous for animals, yet during most of the period a large part of the continent was very quiet. Shallow inland seas from time to time covered a large part of the country. In one of those seas a coral reef was formed at a place now occupied by Louisville, Kentucky. The Ohio River flows over this reef, which is so large that it causes rapids in that stream.

9

The Carboniferous Period

When we studied the different kinds of gases in Chapter 2, we learned that coal is made of atoms of C or carbon, and in Chapter 3 we learned how the chlorophyll in leaves kept the C it took from the CO_2. Our first great coal beds were made in the period that we are now going to talk about. It has, therefore, been named the Carboniferous Period. It began, perhaps, about 280 million years ago and lasted about 50 million years.

Coal beds are made from peat bogs, and peat bogs are made from fallen trees, branches, and even leaves. In order to have peat bogs, however, there must be a great deal of low marshy country; you could never have a peat bog on top of a hill. Peat bogs are formed on low flat land near an ocean or lake. When the leaves, branches, and even the trunks of the trees fall into the swamp, they partly decay and crumble into small pieces and become what we call peat, and swamps of this kind are called peat bogs. When peat is dried, it will burn slowly in a fireplace, and for this reason our great-grandparents a hundred years ago or so used to dig peat and burn it as we now burn coal. In the Carboniferous Period the land was covered with dense forests of very tall treelike growths, which in the course of time fell and formed huge peat bogs, which finally gave us the coal we find so useful.

Figure 9-1 is a picture of a typical swamp forest in the Carboniferous Period. During this period there were vast swamps covered with these great forests. The air was warm and moist so that the trees grew rapidly. It was summer weather even in Greenland, and these huge trees grew there in those days; their fossil forms have been discovered by geologists. When a tree fell down, its place was quickly taken by new growth. The swamps, therefore, soon became filled with partly decayed wood, and new trees grew on the rubbish of the old forests. Nyora Gully, in Australia, (Figure 9-2), is a living example of what such a forest might have been like. Of course, this is not a Carboniferous forest; nevertheless, compare it with Figure 9-1.

In this period the trees of the forests grew close together and had become tall, sometimes one hundred feet or more high, but they were very different from the trees you are used to seeing. Besides the tall, treelike ferns of Devonian time, there were now added to the forest some new and strange varieties, which increased the weird effect of Carboniferous scenery.

Sigillaria (Figure 9-1) lived only in this period, but by their size and numbers they must have contributed greatly to our coal beds. One fossil Sigillaria has been found that was six feet in diameter near the foot of the tree, and another one which measured one hundred feet from end to end.

Very close cousins of Sigillaria were members of a group called Lepidodendron (Figure 9-1), which also grew to be one hundred feet high but had more slender trunks. Lepidodendron, unlike Sigillaria, developed many branches, but the leaves clung to the trunk and the main branches so that they appeared as if they were scaly. This tree was a little more

Figure 9-1. This is a forest in the Carboniferous Period. From these swamps came peat bogs and then our coal beds. Two trees that contributed greatly to our coal beds are Sigillaria and Lepidodendron shown in the clump at the left. Calamites is at the right. (© *Chicago Natural History Museum*)

PLANTS
Club Mosses — Numbers 1-13
Seed Ferns — Numbers 14-16
Ferns — Numbers 17-19
Jointed-Stem Plants —
    Numbers 20-21
Gymnosperms — Number 22

INSECTS (Numbers 23-26)
Notice particularly the early
    dragonflies — Number 24

VERTEBRATES
Primitive Amphibia —
    Numbers 27-29

hardy than the Sigillaria, for it survived into the next period, when it perished.

The most important trees that appeared in this period had the name Cordaites. They were the forerunners of the "big trees" of California, the giant sequoias and redwoods (Figure 9-3). Our own pine trees and spruce trees are also derived from this early group of Cordaites.

The small plants that we now call club mosses and horsetails were then huge trees or at least descended from the cousins of the Lepidodendron and calamites (Figure 9-1).

Then the earth's crust did some more wrinkling, and some of these great swamp forests sank a little, so that water drained in and shallow inland seas formed where the trees had grown. In the course of time, they became covered with mud and sand and sank farther down into the crust of the earth. It was hot down there — very hot — for the farther you go down into the earth, the hotter it gets. The peat formed by these fallen tree trunks was baked so thoroughly that there was almost nothing left but carbon. This was the carbon that had been taken from the air when the chlorophyll in the leaves of the trees absorbed the CO_2 from the air, kept the atoms of C, and let the atoms of O go free. Carbon from the old peat bogs that has been baked in this way we call coal.

Many times, after a peat bog had sunk, it was covered with enough mud to reach to the surface of the water. Then a new forest grew on this second swamp and there was formed another peat bog, which in its turn sank and became coal. Of course when the peat was pressed and baked into coal, the layers of mud were, at the same time and for the same reason, turned into rock. Sometimes the land rose again sufficiently to bring these beds of coal near the surface. Thus, as we dig into the ground, we occasionally find several beds of coal and,

Figure 9-2. No, this is not an ancient Carboniferous forest. It exists now in Australia; the trees are modern. But if it were not disturbed for a million years, it might make a coal bed.

(Australian News and Information Bureau)

between these beds, layers of rock, which had once been ancient mud.

When we put tons of coal into the cellar to burn in the furnace, it is interesting to think how long it took the Carboniferous forests to make the peat that was baked into this coal. It has been estimated that it took many centuries to make the peat for even a narrow seam of coal. Still more time was required to cover that peat bog with mud and to sink and bake it far down in the earth.

While they were alive, those vast forests were a wonderful home for new varieties of fauna. Lepidodendron and Cordaites, and their associates in the forests, were the first trees to

Figure 9-3.   Some of the tallest and oldest trees on the earth, the sequoias and redwoods, are found in the forests of California, Oregon, and Washington.   (Southern Pacific Photo)

shelter the forerunners of the true dragonflies living today. In those days the dragonfly-like insect was an imposing creature. To the smaller insects he must have seemed as large as an airship does to us. Some of these "dragonflies" had bodies one and a half feet long and a spread of wings of twenty-nine inches. But at the same time and in the same forest there were tiny "dragonflies" with wings only half an inch from tip to tip.

The ancient and well-known families of cockroaches, grasshoppers, and locusts appeared during this period. Of course they were all in a somewhat primitive state from our point of view. Yet, after all, they have changed surprisingly little in the last 200 million years.

Centipedes also flourished, for a fossil one was found at Mazon Creek, Illinois, that was twelve inches long and three-quarters of an inch thick. Some of its great compound eyes contained a thousand lenses.

Another emergence from the sea during the Carboniferous Period was that of the familiar land snail. It probably isn't correct to imagine the first snail swimming through the surf, galloping up on the beach, and shouting to the first settler, "Scorpion! I am here." As with the other air-breathing fauna, its coming out of the sea and changing from the water-dwelling stage to the land-life stage must have been a long and dangerous experience.

Meanwhile, the descendants of early amphibians had grown so numerous that they had to earn a living in very different ways. Some were adapted to spending a large part of their time in the water. For such a purpose it was advantageous to have a long, slim body, which could slip through the water easily; so, according to the well-known law of nature, some began to develop such shapes. Others stayed more and more on land and developed their legs for walking. Some of these amphibians were ten feet long and others were only six inches from head to tail. At Linton, Ohio, underneath a coal bed, the fossils of over fifty different kinds of amphibians of this period have been found. Apparently, they had at different times got stuck in a peat swamp, died there, and were finally buried by peat. Then when the peat was baked into coal, they were baked into fossils.

Some fauna appeared during the millions of years of this Carboniferous Period that have always been very peaceful and unwarlike and that we, as well as the starfish, find very good to eat. They have been contented with sea life and have not tried to crawl up on the land. We call them oysters. Remember that the first primitive oyster appeared in this period along with the coal with which we now cook his descendants.

It is interesting to think how the map of North America looked during this period and how it had changed from the Devonian map as well as how it differed from the North America of today. If an amphibian of this age had wanted to, he could have crawled not only to Greenland but to Europe, for there was land all the way. Instead of finding great fields of ice, he would have crawled through fine forests of such trees as calamites and Sigillaria. He would probably have had to dodge some of those foot-and-a-half dragonflies and to have been careful not to disturb one of those Illinois centipedes. If he went by the coast, he would have been wise not to swim too far into deep water, for there were many sharks in those seas.

The long, narrow sea, which, during part of the last or Devonian Period, stretched from the water we now call the Gulf of Mexico to Newfoundland, is gone. Its place is nearly all taken by dry land, and the only water is the irregularly shaped inland sea, consisting mostly of swamps, that extended across the Mississippi Valley and south to Mexico.

During the middle Devonian the land at that place had

begun to rise. The earth's crust had wrinkled again, and since this valley, filled with water, was the weakest place in this part of the world, the first wrinkle appeared here. The first effect of the slow folding of the crust was the raising of the bottom of this narrow sea. If fishes had been swimming in those days up and down this body of water, they would have found that the sea was becoming more shallow. Finally rocks would have appeared above the water. At last, those fishes of the inland sea would have lost their water and suffocated on the dry land that came in its place.

The crust of the earth moves so slowly that it is hard to imagine how long it took the bottom of this shallow sea to rise and make dry land. We think of the Egyptians as living in the very remote past — six thousand years ago or so; but it probably required more than six million years to turn this inland sea into dry land.

During the next period the crust kept on folding until a great mountain range miles high had risen where this inland sea had been. What is left of these magnificent folds we call the Appalachian Mountains. Thus the earth is ever changing, and sometimes very tiny movements that can hardly be noticed are the forerunners of mighty events in the history of geography; but before we can learn about that, we will have to study in the next chapter about one of the most curious and interesting things in nature.

10

Ice Ages

We must first describe some very cold times that occasionally cover the earth with ice. It was during the period after the Carboniferous that one of these cold ages occurred, and since, on at least seven other occasions, a large part of the earth has been covered with ice, we will devote this entire chapter to a description of these strange happenings. We call such a cold time an Ice Age.

The world is so interesting and so full of strange things that, when we start to tell a story about an Ice Age, it is hard to decide just where we should begin. Let us commence with ice and try to find out what ice is and how it behaves.

We all know that when water is very cold, it freezes and becomes ice. This happens at a temperature that we call 32°. If you place a thermometer in ice-water and stir the water so that all the parts will be of the same temperature, the end of the little mercury column should be at exactly 32°. This is one way of testing the accuracy of a thermometer, for if the end of the mercury column is one degree higher, that is 33°, or one degree lower, 31°, then you will know that the thermometer is not just right.

Water is not the only thing that freezes. Almost everything freezes, and everything that does has a special temperature at which it becomes frozen or at which it melts. Most things around us are frozen or solid all the time; for example, candles, lead, iron, glass, and rock are usually in this frozen condition when we see them. If you have a very hot fire, you can melt lead. Then you will find that it melts at 617°. We can say that water freezes into ice at 32° and that melted lead freezes into solid lead at 617°. When liquid lava pours out of a volcano, it is very hot. The air is so much colder that the lava quickly freezes and becomes what we call rock, which is then just frozen lava. However, we are now more interested in frozen water and the way it behaves when a great deal of it is made.

When you look at snowflakes that have fallen on some dark cloth, you will find that they are made of a great many very tiny crystals of ice. Before they melt, you can sometimes see them through a magnifying glass. Then you will find that these tiny crystals make very beautiful patterns (Figure 10-1). These crystals are just frozen particles of water.

Figure 10-1. If you have a microscope or powerful magnifying glass, you will spend enjoyable hours examining snowflakes. They are made up of beautiful crystals of ice, like the one above. *(American Museum of Natural History)*

You know how wet fog is. That is because it consists of little particles of water that are just as round as tiny balls. Each particle is so small that it is invisible to the naked eye. When the air is full of these little particles, it is hard to see through it, and we then say it is a foggy day. Sometimes the fog is formed high up in the sky, and then we call it a cloud. When these little particles of water become crowded together in a cloud, they will hit each other and join together to form larger particles. Finally, they get so large that the air cannot any longer hold them up in the sky and they fall down to the earth. Of course everything under that cloud gets wet and we say it is raining.

When it is very cold up in the sky — less than 32° Fahrenheit — then the little particles of water freeze into those tiny crystals that you saw on the dark cloth, and when they get crowded and come together, they form snowflakes and fall to the ground. It is so cold on the tops of some high mountains that all clouds blowing over them become snowflakes and keep the tops of the mountains covered with snow and ice all the time. You may wonder where the ice comes from that is on top of a mountain when only snowflakes have fallen there. It is made from snowflakes, for when they are packed together in great piles and are very cold, they become one solid block of ice like the frozen water in our ponds in winter.

Ice behaves in a very curious way. If you hit it with a hammer, it will crack and break like glass. On the other hand, if you leave the hammer on top of a block of ice, after a while it will begin to sink into the ice without a crack or a break. That is, if you press against ice hard and for a long time, it will bend just like putty; but if you hit it a sharp blow, it will crack and break.

Ice is not alone in being so peculiar. Candles, glass, rock, and many other things behave in this way. You have probably seen a candle in warm weather keep bending very slowly until after several weeks it was pointing downward instead of up. Yet during all that time, if you had given that candle a sudden blow, it would have cracked and broken. A long glass tube will bend if you handle it gently, but as you well know, it will break if you strike it suddenly. Those great wrinkles in the earth that formed the mountains were made so slowly that the rock for miles would usually just bend without breaking or cracking. Of course sometimes the rock does crack like a windowpane, and then the land in the neighborhood trembles, and we call it an earthquake. But usually the land bends so slowly that it takes millions of years to form a wrinkle. Some parts of North America are bending now, but the movement is so slow that even the change made in a hundred years would have to be measured by an expert.

Again let us return to the ice that has been formed by countless millions of snowflakes high up in the mountains. This ice at first rests just where it was made on the steep slope of the mountain. Like everything else on a steep slope, if nothing prevented, it would slide down to the bottom of the mountain. In this case it cannot slide at once, for it is frozen into all the rough and uneven places in the rock surface. However, that tendency to slide to the bottom is always there; so the ice slowly yields as it did to the hammer that started sinking into the block. Little by little that great mass of ice moves toward the bottom of the mountain. As the top of the ice begins to move down like the candle, the bottom, which is frozen into the cracks and rough surfaces, is forced to come along also. If the mass of ice is very large — perhaps hundreds of feet thick — the force of it is so great that the bottom is carried right along with the top. The great weight of the ice breaks away all the rough places in the rock and carries all this debris down to the foot of the mountain. Such a great moving mass of ice sliding down the side of a mountain is called a glacier (Figure 10-2).

Glaciers move very slowly, for it takes ice a long time to bend into new shapes and flow down the sides of a mountain and then out over the land. Many travel only a few feet a day, although there is one in Greenland that moves sixty feet a day. When the glaciers reach the ocean as they sometimes do in Greenland, Alaska, and on the shores of the Antarctic Continent, great blocks of ice break off and float out to sea (Figure 10-3). These floating pieces are called icebergs. They rise sometimes a couple of hundred feet from the surface of the water (Figure 10-4). They are very dangerous, for occasionally in a fog ships run into them and sink.

Figure 10-2.   This beautiful river of ice is a glacier sliding down a mountain.
(Swissair — Photo A.-G. Zürich)

Figure 10-3. If you observe carefully, you will see a great block of ice, an iceberg, breaking off from the glacier. This glacier, in Greenland, is five miles wide at its mouth, and the iceberg is one mile across at the point where it is breaking off.   *(U.S. Coast Guard Official Photo)*

The amazing thing about an iceberg is that there is usually nine times more ice under water than you can see above water. What we can see of an iceberg is so large, it is hard to imagine how much bigger it really is. If they were standing on the ground, some would be as large as a city block and as tall as a thirty-story building. When such a giant mass breaks

Figure 10-4.   Only a small part of the "berg" is above water, but this may be the longest, thinnest part of the mass, which projects like the apex of a floating cone. This picture was taken by a Coast Guard photographer on a reconnaissance flight over the Grand Banks area.

(U.S. Coast Guard Official Photo)

off from the glacier and plunges into the ocean, it makes a sound like thunder and can be heard for miles around. Such huge waves rise when the giant berg is launched into the sea that it is dangerous for a vessel to go nearer than a mile. It almost seems as if the iceberg were celebrating its joyous return to the sea, for in the first place the sun had evaporated the sea water and made those tiny balls of water that, massed together, floated through the air as enormous fleecy clouds. Then these clouds were blown high in the air over the mountains and turned into crystals of ice that formed snowflakes, which then fell on the mountain and slowly formed that great glacier. Finally the glacier had moved down to the water and a big piece had broken off and slid into the ocean. Sometimes it takes a long time to melt one of these icebergs. They float from Greenland far down into the Atlantic before the ice melts and the tiny balls of water again join their mother ocean.

A great quantity of water is always being held prisoner by these glaciers and ice fields at the North Pole and the South Pole and on the tops of the high mountains. It has been said that if all this ice were melted so that all the tiny balls of water could again be in the sea, the oceans would be so full that our beaches would be entirely under water. The water would even flow through the streets of many of our cities that are near the coast, such as San Francisco, New Orleans, Charleston, and New York. A large part of New Jersey, Florida, Louisiana, and Texas would be under water if such a thing happened.

It is interesting to remember that for millions of years in the Carboniferous Period there were no ice fields and no glaciers even at the North Pole. Instead of icebergs, Greenland in those days produced wonderful forests that made peat bogs and coal beds. Perhaps some day this will happen again. People will then live near the North Pole and have flower gardens, and those living in the cities on the coast will have to build their houses on higher land. Of course, if this state of things ever does come, it will come very slowly and take tens of thousands of years, which will give us plenty of time to prepare for it.

It is interesting in this connection to remember that during most of the history of the earth for the last 1,000 million years — that is, before our own history commences — Greenland was a warm and delightful place in which to live. Such a condition in Greenland seems to be the normal state, so that probably some day, perhaps 30,000 years from now, great cities will be built throughout Greenland where now the ice is perhaps a mile thick.

When great rocks or boulders from the sides of the mountain fall on glaciers, they gradually sink through the ice to the bottom, and then they not only scratch the sides of the mountain but actually grind it into dust and wear it away, for the enormous weight of the ice, pressing on these boulders embedded in it, actually scrapes the rock as if it were clay. At the entrance to the American Museum of Natural History in New York City, there is a large flat rock that has been not only scratched but quite deeply grooved by a glacier. The rocks that were carried down by the glacier were also often scratched. Like most glacial rocks the edges have been worn round because the rocks have been scraped and rolled over the bottom of the valley. The water that flows from the end of a glacier is so full of fine particles of rock that it looks gray. In the course of ages glaciers dig great valleys in the sides of mountains.

Sometimes in the past ages of the earth a glacier was so large that it flowed like a mass of cold molasses far out upon the land. Such a sheet of ice has been known to be a mile thick, so that it flowed right over all hills and even all but the highest mountains. We can now tell where it has been by finding scratches on the rocks of today (Figure 10-5). The direction in which these scratches point shows the path over which the glacier flowed. Where the glacier ended, there are

Figure 10-5. Glacial scratches, running nearly horizontally over this smooth rock, were made by boulders embedded in the ice at the bottom of the glacier that once covered this ledge.

(N.Y. State Museum and Science Service)

often great piles of rocks and gravel, which were dropped by the ice as it finally melted.

If a season grew warmer after one of these ice ages, so that rain instead of snow fell on the glacier, rivers would be formed. After a short time these rivers would cut deep canyons in the ice and flow like a mountain torrent between great cliffs of ice or through tunnels in the ice. All the sand, pebbles, and even boulders that had been collected by the glacier would be carried by these streams out into the open country and spread on the land. We find today all over the northern part of North America such mounds, and even hills of gravel and boulders, which were piled up by the last glacier that covered the land.

Glaciers change the shape of the valleys through which they flow. Nearly all valleys are first made by rivers. They are narrow at the bottom and wide at the top, much like the letter V. After a glacier has ground and scoured the bottom of a valley for 100,000 years, it presents a very different appearance. The bottom becomes wide and the sides very steep. The valleys pictured in Figures 10-6 and 10-7 were once V-shaped valleys that have been scoured and rounded by glaciers.

We don't know why these great ice fields came and covered whole countries with glaciers a mile thick. Also we don't know why warm weather came again and melted the fields of ice. Perhaps it was because the earth wrinkled so much in some places and the land rose so high that it snowed during the whole year and then year after year. The ice that was formed in those places would never have a chance to melt and would grow deeper and deeper. Finally, it would spread in all directions until it covered whole countries. When perhaps after 100,000 years the land sank again or was worn down by the grinding of the ice, it would rain instead of snow and would melt the glacier by forming those great canyons through which the rivers rushed and carried boulders and sand with them.

Some think that an ice age is caused by a change in the amount of heat that the sun is giving us. They say that for some unknown reason the sun is sometimes a little brighter and sometimes a little fainter. Its being a little fainter for hundreds of thousands of years might cause an ice age.

Figure 10-6.   This valley was scarred by a glacier. Once it was V-shaped.
(U.S. Geological Survey)

Perhaps some day the true cause of an ice age will be discovered and you will read about it in the newspapers and magazines.

Figure 10-7. Yosemite Valley, California, with El Capitan on the left and Cathedral Rocks on the right. Before the glacier came, this valley was narrow with steep sides like the letter V. Then the glacier ground away the rocks and made the valley wide and round like the letter U.

(Union Pacific Railroad Photo)

11

The Permian Period

Nearly a hundred years ago an English scientist was asked by the Czar of Russia to study the rocks of the Ural Mountains. In this way the rock record of the period of earth history next after the Carboniferous Period was discovered. Because it was in the province of Perm, in Russia, they called this the Permian Period. By "rock record" we don't mean that there were any words carved in the stone, but some things tell a story to scientists just as well as if whole pages had been written. For example, if you found the skeleton of the earliest amphibian or any of his family, you would know that the rocks in which the skeleton was buried must have been mud in the Devonian Period, for you remember that it was in that period that the first amphibians made their appearance. This reading of the story of the earth from the rocks is very interesting.

The Permian Period began some 230 million years ago and lasted for perhaps 25 million years. This period was important for the descendants of the earliest amphibians. They learned many tricks in those millions of years of which the old fellow never dreamed.

In the first place, one of those great ice ages occurred

during this period. Perhaps it was the greatest ice age the earth has ever known. The ice covered most of South Africa, nearly all of India, and parts of Australia. Now you think of Brazil as a very warm country, but during the Permian Period there were ice sheets on its Atlantic coast even close to what is now the Amazon River. In North America there was a huge glacier where Boston now is and another over a part at least of the Gulf of St. Lawrence.

The forests that grew in the nice warm air of that Carboniferous Period were suffering from winter weather that had not visited the earth before for millions of years. The great forest trees of Sigillaria, Lepidodendron, and calamites, which helped to make the peat bogs that in turn became coal beds, couldn't stand the cold and died in large numbers. Some survived the cold but were not as successful as they might have been. At present, as you know, the survivors of this family are merely weeds — club mosses and horsetails. If you want to see trees stunted today by cold weather, all you need to do is to climb a mountain or travel far into northern Canada, Labrador, or Alaska. When you climb a mountain, the higher you get, the shorter you will find the trees, for it is increasingly cold as you climb higher and higher up the mountains. After a while you will get so high that it will be too cold and windy for even short trees, and you will find then only bushes and weeds. Then as you climb on, if the mountain is very high, you will leave all the bushes behind and come to only moss-covered rocks. Even moss can't live when it is too cold and windy, so you next find just plain rocks. Finally, on the very top you find that you are up in the sky among the clouds and that the ground all about you is covered with snow and ice. In the Permian Period the great fields of ice cooled the air so much that the trees grew smaller just as if the land had risen like a mountain.

Among the trees there was an energetic family that we have mentioned before, the family of Cordaites (Figure 9-1). The Cordaites appeared to be adapted to many conditions, and some survived the cold climate. Some have continued to grow even to the present time. The "big trees" of California were developed at this time and are descended from this very independent and progressive family of Cordaites, as we learned when we read about the Carboniferous Period. You remember also that the spruce, firs, pine trees, and the great redwood trees of Oregon and Washington are cousins of the sequoia or "big trees," and all appeared at this time, taking the place of the fast-dying Carboniferous trees.

Trees were not the only forms of life that had to struggle to survive the cold of the glacial period. Those big dragonflies of the Carboniferous Period weren't adapted to the cold and finally all perished in the Permian Period. The little dragonflies and some other insects (Figure 11-1) were apparently

Figure 11-1.   Dunbaria is the name of this beautifully preserved insect that lived in Kansas during the early part of the Permian Period. The color bands are plainly visible on the wings. It was found among the rocks of Insect Hill near Elmo, Kansas, by C. O. Dunbar of Yale University and was described and named by R. J. Tillyard of Australia.

(Peabody Museum, Yale University)

tougher and so did not die out, for you have seen many of them flying about over ponds and streams. They are mainly descended from the tough little dragonflies of the Carboniferous Period.

Down in Australia scientists have found a fossil beetle that lived during this period. He is the oldest beetle ever discovered. Like his descendants of today, he could survive the snowy winters and live in the neighborhood of great glaciers. His hard skin and ways of living were so well adapted to all kinds of weather that we have beetles now looking much like their old Permian ancestor.

The great glaciers on the shores of the continents must have filled the oceans with huge icebergs many times bigger than our present icebergs. Some of these glaciers were a mile thick. When they reached the ocean, blocks of ice a mile high fell into the sea. No ship today ever saw such icebergs. Some of these bergs with pointed peaks like mountains may have risen one thousand feet above the waves of the sea. That would be twice as high as the Washington Monument. They would have extended many thousand feet under the water. It would have been a journey of miles to sail around one of those islands of ice.

No wonder the ocean grew cold as well as the land, so that the sea dwellers had as hard a time as the calamites and Sigillaria. Those huge sea scorpions that began their family history in the Silurian Period found the environment too harsh, and one by one, like many animals without backbones, they died and were eaten by their enemies. However, some humble cousins of these six-foot sea scorpions were more lively and stayed. They were a little different in shape, too, but still the family resemblance was very strong. These smaller fellows developed finally into forms that survive to the present day and make a very popular food for all of us. In the Mesozoic we began to recognize some of these survivors as lobsters and some of them as crabs.

In the world of fishes a very important change took place during this period. While the water was warm and food was plentiful, a fish could earn a living even if he had a clumsy tail, for heretofore the backbone extended way down to one end of a fish's tail. You can see in Figure 11-2 what a clumsy-looking tail this made. In this period, however, the clumsy forms that were the ancestors of the living sharks and rays begin to disappear. In fresh water, the riphidistians that were ancestors of our amphibians had already disappeared, and now late in the Permian ray-finned fishes have invaded the seas. So after millions of years most of the fishes that survived had the well-shaped tails that are the pride of our own fishes.

Figure 11-2.   When you have the opportunity, examine the tail of a modern fish. Silurian fishes, however, had this characteristic tail.

(American Museum of Natural History)

These hard times were caused not only by the cold winds from the glaciers and the oceans with many icebergs, but also by new wrinklings of the earth, which made huge mountains rise. You remember that in the Silurian Period there was a long, narrow sea extending from the Gulf of Mexico to Newfoundland. Then in the Devonian Period the land rose so that this sea became shallow and there were mountains in the place we now call New England. During this Permian Period this land continued to rise until there came those wrinkles in the crust that now we call the Appalachian Mountains. In those days when the mountains were young, they were much higher than now. Some of the peaks were perhaps more than three miles high. The land at that time extended far out into the Atlantic Ocean, and nearly all of North America had risen so high that all inland seas except one had drained off. Nevertheless, this sea covered that part of the country now called New Mexico, Arizona, Texas, Nevada, and California.

North of this sea was a land of many volcanoes. They are not there now, but in those days these volcanoes sent rivers of hot lava far out upon the land.

You will not be surprised then to learn that the amphibians were having a hard struggle to live. Figure 11-3 is a picture of some of these amphibians. Some were nine feet long and others only six inches long. Their favorite swamps of the Carboniferous Period had become dry land, so that they had to live on the banks of rivers or on the edge of that sea that covered the state of Utah. Some amphibians were therefore crowded out of the water and forced to hunt for their food on land far from the sea. That was a difficult thing for them to do. They had always crawled on the land and dragged their stomachs on the ground. In the search for food in the forest, those that could travel only in this slow way went hungry. Probably many of this distinguished family died from starvation, because they had been crowded out of the rivers, and in dark forests they were too slow to catch bugs. Fortunately for us, some neither starved nor stayed on the riverbanks. These were the amphibians that happened to have stronger feet; they could move faster. This was a great advantage, and in

Figure 11-3.   At the beginning of the Permian Period, the Amphibia had developed into a variety of forms. Cricotus was probably known among his associates as a famous swimmer. Cacops was too stout for his length. Eryops was noted for having a head that was almost solid. The best we can say for them all is that they were probably just a little brighter than fishes. After a drawing by W. K. Gregory and Richard Deckert at the American Museum of Natural History.   (*American Museum of Natural History*)

the course of millions of years a race of strong-footed creatures was developed, for in each generation the best runner got the most food, while many of the slow ones starved. Finally, these creatures learned to live on land and to breathe air exclusively and never went near the water. But most important, they laid eggs in which the young embryo was protected against drying out. We call them reptiles (Figure 11-4). For about 160 million years the reptiles were the most powerful animals in the world.

Although the change from the amphibian to the reptile was very gradual and took millions of years, yet we think of one reptilian type as resembling the "founder" of the group.

Figure 11-4.   Some primitive reptiles of the Permian Period. Jonkeria and
Lycaenops fed on animals. The other three acted strangely for reptiles;
they ate plants. But after all they were primitive and had amphibians as
ancestors.   *(American Museum of Natural History)*

He may have looked like Labidosaurus (Figure 11-5). Since
he represents one of our remote ancestors and the founder of
a new era in our family history, we should hang his portrait
in our dining-room beside that of our earliest amphibian
ancestor.

Like all families, the descendants of the Labidosaurus-type
reptile moved into many countries and began to live in varied
ways. This finally made them look different from each other,

Figure 11-5.   Labidosaurus, a reptile that lived in Texas during the Permian Period. He was about four feet long.

(American Museum of Natural History)

and each had his own pet form of behavior (Figure 11-6). Some began to have heads like dogs (Figure 11-7). You might say that their teeth appear to be more like those of a dog or cat than like those of a reptile, and teeth are a very important part of any reptile. These reptiles are called "beast-shaped." They were the most intelligent animals that so far had come upon the earth, and it was this branch of the reptile family that in a very indirect fashion was perhaps closely related to our ancestors. However, they were reptiles, and while their teeth were differently shaped, they were still reptile teeth, not dogs' or cats' teeth.

The amount of brains that an animal has is fairly well indicated by the way in which he gets his food. In all ages the animals that kill and eat other animals or that can escape quickly are usually brighter and quicker than the ones content to eat only leaves and grass and to move slowly. It appears to require more brains to catch an amphibian and conquer him than to eat plants. In the course of time the brightest, quickest, and bravest of the meat eaters learned how to catch a variety of animals. Such were the beast-shaped reptiles of which the Scymnognathus (Figure 11-7) was a good example. Just as the reptiles were brighter and stronger than

Figure 11-6.   A Permian scene. Which are the reptiles? Which are the amphibians?   (© *Chicago Natural History Museum*)

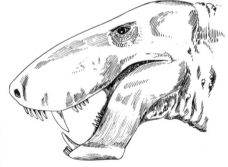

Figure 11-7.   Scymnognathus, a dog-toothed reptile related to the ancestors of the mammals. After a drawing by W. K. Gregory and Richard Deckert at the American Museum of Natural History. (*American Museum of Natural History*)

the amphibians, so after millions of years the beast-shaped reptiles were the brightest and strongest of all the reptiles.

Before the end of the period some of the reptiles had developed most unusual forms (Figure 11-8). There were, for instance, "fin-backed" reptiles, savage creatures that killed and ate not only amphibians and smaller reptiles, but perhaps each other. We do not know what use they had for those high fins on their backs.

We ought not to leave the Permian Period without mentioning the salt beds of Kansas and Germany. The movement of the land drained, and the dryness of the air evaporated many lakes and inland seas. The gradual drying of a large inland sea or lake made smaller salt lakes. You remember how Lake Bonneville gradually dried up and grew smaller

Figure 11-8.   About 200 million years ago Dimetrodon with bright eyes and smiling mouth had this magnificent fin back. He belonged to the ruling class of reptiles then flourishing in what is now Texas.

(American Museum of Natural History)

until it formed our present Great Salt Lake in Utah. In Kansas, in the course of thousands of years salt beds two hundred feet thick were formed and buried far down beneath the surface of the earth. When wells are bored into the ground, these salt beds are found over an area of about 100,000 square miles. It is estimated that they contain thousands of millions of tons of salt — the greatest mass of salt that has ever been discovered in the earth. The next greatest salt beds are in Germany. In some places these beds are three thousand feet thick.

Some beds of salt have been mined for hundreds of years. There is a famous salt mine in Austria where handsome rooms have been carved in the rock salt.

12

The Triassic Period

The next three periods are sometimes called the Age of Reptiles. During this age the reptiles became very numerous and powerful. For over 100 million years they ruled the air, land, and sea. They learned to fly and swim. Some that stayed on the land became the biggest, heaviest fauna that have ever lived on the earth. You remember that these reptiles came into existence at the time of great disturbances. There were earthquakes; glaciers a mile thick were spreading over the land; huge icebergs were floating in the ocean; and the land was rising and drying up the swamps when Labidosaurus lived. His descendants failed to adapt to changing conditions, or so scientists think. They became very set in their ways, and after 100 million years or more they became a bit old-fashioned. Then another of the earth's revolutions came and utterly destroyed them. It is odd that, having been born as it were in one revolution, they couldn't stand another.

The next period, and the first of the Age of Reptiles, is called the Triassic. It began perhaps 205 million years ago and lasted about 40 million years. All the ice of the Permian Period had disappeared, and during most of this time the air was warm and dry even near the North Pole, and there were dense forests in northern Greenland. In Virginia and North Carolina there were giant ferns, and the tall sequoias and redwood trees grew all over our continent as they do now in California, Oregon, and Washington. A Triassic landscape is to be seen in Figure 12-1.

Figure 12-1.   A Triassic landscape, with characteristic ferns.
(American Museum of Natural History)

Some of these great trees fell into an inland sea and floated
south to Arizona, where they were buried in the mud. After
millions of years in the ground they were turned to stone.
Then the overlying rocks were gradually worn away, and now
in Arizona we can see the stone trunks of these trees lying
on the ground. Some are eight feet in diameter and 120 feet
long. The government has set aside this land as a national
park (Figure 12-2).

Although the reptiles ruled most of the land, they were not
at peace. They fought with each other and even ate each

Figure 12-2.   These petrified stumps of tree trunks may have had their
origin in the Triassic.   *(National Park Service)*

other. Some reptiles became adapted to living in the sea. Some developed hard shells to protect themselves against their enemies. Figure 12-3 is a picture of one of these old reptiles that returned to a seafaring life. He may have been similar to the ancestor of our turtles, sometimes called chelonians.

Figure 12-3.   Placochelys, a reptile, adapted to a seafaring life. Does he remind you of a turtle? There is some thought that animals like him were the ancestors of our turtles.   *(American Museum of Natural History)*

Members of another branch of the reptile family that were obliged to return to the water in order to get food are called plesiosaurs (Figure 12-4). At the end of the Age of Reptiles they perished. No one knows why this happened; perhaps they couldn't stand the cold period. Therefore, they are not our ancestors. They are merely some poor relatives who failed in the struggle for existence.

During the fierce struggle for survival, some reptiles were pushed farther and farther into the sea until finally only those survived that could live in the water. Their shapes were very much changed, as you can see from the picture of one of them (Figure 12-5). They are called ichthyosaurs, which means fish-lizards. They roamed the sea and killed many

Figure 12-4. At the left Plesiosaurus takes a swim, while a relative of his hunts for his meal.   *(American Museum of Natural History)*

Figure 12-5.   A Triassic ichthyosaur. He had a very interesting family tree of ancestors. Far back in the Silurian Period his ancestors were fishes. In the Devonian Period they partly left the water and became amphibians. In the early part of the Permian Period they left the water entirely and became reptiles. They returned to the banks of the streams and behaved like amphibians. Finally in the Triassic Period Cymbospondylus stayed in the water all the time and behaved like his remote ancestors, the fishes. After a drawing by W. K. Gregory and Richard Deckert of the American Museum of Natural History.   *(American Museum of Natural History)*

large fish. We will meet them again before we finish with this
Age of Reptiles.

The most interesting reptiles were those that had become
adapted to walk on their hind legs. They and certain of their
relatives who walked on all four legs are called dinosaurs.
Coelophysis (Figure 12-6) may be considered to be the
founder or "stem" reptile of the dinosaur group. In a fascinat-
ing book called *Evolution in the Past*, by H. R. Knipe, an
English scientist, it is recorded that Plato, a famous Greek
philosopher, who lived about two thousand years ago, once
tried to describe man in such a way as to show how he differed from all other animals. He finally concluded that the
two things that made a man different from all other forms of
life were that he had no feathers and that he walked on two

Figure 12-6.   Coelophysis, a reptile that might have been a stem-reptile, or
founder, of the dinosaur group.   *(American Museum of Natural History)*

feet. Of course Plato had never heard of Anchisaurus, who exactly fits this description.

Some of the descendants of either Coelophysis or his contemporaries developed into vegetarians. After millions of years the dinosaurs that were meat eaters became very different from their cousins who ate leaves and plants. When a dinosaur who ate flora was hungry, he walked up to a bush and began eating. He could walk as slowly as he pleased, for the bush wouldn't run away from him; also, the bush wouldn't fight to defend itself. Figure 12-7 is a picture of one of these vegetable eaters, named Plateosaurus, whose ancestors had given up their meat diet. Before the Age of Reptiles was over, these plant eaters grew to an immense size. Some weighed 80,000 pounds and were tall enough to have eaten from the roof of a two-story house. In a later chapter we will learn more about them and how they perished at the close of the Age of Reptiles.

Figure 12-7. This is a picture of Plateosaurus. He was one of the most peaceful dinosaurs that lived and ate only bushes and plants. His hind legs show the thick and heavy "elephant" leg.

(American Museum of Natural History)

No great range of mountains rose during the Triassic Period. However, the land was far from being quiet and peaceful. All along the Pacific coastal region of North America from California to Alaska volcanoes spouted flames and ashes high in the air and rivers of hot lava flowed down their sides. An inland sea covered the part of the country now called California, Oregon, Washington, and British Columbia, and from this water rose countless volcanoes. The lava from these volcanoes can still be found on the land in those places. Now of course, that coastal land is no longer there, for millions of years ago it disappeared into the depths of the ocean.

The North Atlantic Coast was also disturbed. Cracks that extended for many miles appeared in the earth. In some places the land on one side of a crack would rise hundreds of feet in the air and the land on the other side would sink equally far, so that great cliffs were formed. From these cracks there sometimes flowed masses of melted rock or lava. When this lava cooled, it often formed long six-sided columns packed close together. They are called basaltic columns. The Palisades on the west bank of the Hudson River were made of basaltic rocks that came out of the earth at this period. At the same time Mount Tom in Massachusetts, the East Rock at New Haven, and Orange Mountain in New Jersey were formed. This series of cliffs, with here and there fairly well-made six-sided columns, extends across Pennsylvania and Maryland to Virginia. The picture of the Devil's Post Pile (Figure 12-8) is an excellent example of these basaltic columns, which in some cases instead of being six-sided are five- and even seven-sided.

In the Triassic Period the land extended far out into the Atlantic Ocean on the east coast of North America, and the land near these cliffs of basaltic columns was dry like a desert.

If you go through this part of the country, you will find a

Figure 12-8.   Devil's Post Pile, National Monument on San Joaquin River, Sierra National Forest, California.   *(National Park Service)*

great deal of red sandstone that was made at this time, for some of the rock contained iron ore, and when particles were worn away and became mud in the valleys, the iron ore made the rock red. Then in time the mud was pressed into rock and became the well-known red sandstone that is so typical of this part of the country. Sometimes you will find footprints of dinosaurs in this red sandstone. A number of these footprints have been cut from the rock in the Connecticut River Valley. One of them is shown in Figure 12-9; it holds enough water, (18 gallons to be precise) so that the little fellow can cool off in it.

The forests during the Triassic Period must have been a wonderful sight. As we said, there were tall sequoia and redwood trees and quantities of cycads (Figure 12-10) that were much like those living today. Few, if any, colored flowers had appeared as yet. You would have missed the birds also, if you had been there, for nothing flew in the air except a few large insects and some dragonflies and a strange flying dragon, which you will learn about in the next chapter.

Figure 12-9. Eighteen gallons of water fit into this footprint of a dinosaur, a reptile. Now it serves as a cooling-off place for a young fellow.
   (Courtesy of Roland T. Bird)

Figure 12-10.   This cycad now is to be found in the Brooklyn Botanic Garden. Its ancestors flourished in the Triassic. *(Brooklyn Botanic Garden)*

If you had looked at the ground under those giant trees and near the cycads, you probably would have found some of those remarkable little creatures that we call ants. They were the first of the fauna to help each other and to divide their work with their neighbors. This was a great event in the history of the earth. Hundreds of millions of years earlier the little individual cells had united into groups and divided the work of living among them. As you probably remember, some cells protected the group with a tough outer layer and others caught the food. It was probably in the Triassic Period that the second step in cooperation was taken, when a little group of ants began helping each other instead of fighting each other. Although the earliest fossil ant so far discovered lived a few periods later (Oligocene), yet it is probable that the ants began their career in this period.

There isn't room in this book to describe the way in which ants live, but they probably lived in the Triassic Period about as they do today. You will read some day how they build houses for each other and hold little aphids as servants, just as we do cows and horses. For some unknown reason the ants never grew large.

While you were looking on the ground at those very intelligent ants in the Triassic forests, you might have heard a rustling under some cycads, and then perhaps you would have seen a very small animal about the size of a squirrel climb up one of those redwood trees for safety. You would have seen one of your ancestors. Up to recently, some scientists thought he was one of the first mammals, if not the first. Dromatherium is his name. Some students of ancient life think he may have been the founder of your group of mammal ancestors. Now he is considered a mammal-like reptile and not a mammal. But the first mammals may have looked like Dromatherium.

As we have said before, a founder of a new line of ancestors didn't suddenly appear in a new form so different from that of his reptilian parents. Dromatherium was almost exactly like his parents, and his parents were almost like his grandparents. The change from the reptile had been very gradual. Millions of years were required to produce this new form. Dromatherium, the founder of this new type, was found in Virginia, and we have found none of the skeletons of his immediate ancestors. He was descended from some cousins of the beast-shaped reptiles that are described in Chapter 11. A picture of this cousin is given in Figure 11-7.

The early mammals were insignificant compared with their enemies, the dinosaurs. However, the mammals had one great advantage that was destined to make them the ruling animals. The mothers nursed their children, who were therefore guarded, fed, and trained while they were young. Reptiles laid eggs and then usually went off and left them. The poor little reptiles had to struggle out of the shells as best they could. Immediately they had to hunt for their food and if possible avoid their enemies. But the mammals in that far-off Triassic Period began to care for their children. At the present time some of the mammals not only train their children at home, but also send them to school and to college, for people are mammals. Cats, dogs, lions, tigers, horses, cows, and our cousins the apes and monkeys are also mammals.

Thus at the end of the Triassic Period we find there had been evolved mammals — the highest type of animal so far produced on the earth. They were the natural result of incessant warfare — of killing and eating. Countless millions of individuals had been sacrificed in this struggle. During all this period of perhaps 800 million years almost every individual met with a tragic death. A few, perhaps, died of old age or of disease; but most jellyfish, fishes, dragonflies, amphibians, and reptiles were killed and eaten by their enemies, and this fierce condition exists today, not only among the fishes, insects, amphibians, and reptiles, but also among the mammals; for tigers, lions, gorillas, and men still fight both for food and for a place in which to live.

13

The Jurassic Period

The next period was determined by the famous English geologist, William Smith, who lived during the early part of the last century. However, the period was named Jurassic by a French geologist, Alexandre Brogniart, because he found in the rocks of the Jura Mountains between France and Switzerland a more complete record of it than had been previously discovered. This period began about 165 million years ago and like the Triassic Period lasted for about 40 million years.

In the preceding period a very important piece of progress took place, for some of the small reptiles became adapted to flight. You remember that back in the Carboniferous Period, about 100 million years earlier, from segmented seaworms had developed the group to which belong the flying creatures known as dragonflies. Then in the Triassic a reptile became adapted to swoop down in flight upon his food. Now in the Jurassic Period flying became more common, for two kinds of reptiles had taken to the air.

Two very queer things happened to some of these reptiles. In the first place their scales turned into feathers, and then the feathers made the wings. It isn't understood just how feathers came to be worn by birds, for we have never found any fossil remains of a bird that had a skin that was partly scales and partly feathers. Perhaps some day you may find such a fossil, and then you can learn just how scales were able to change to feathers. Reptiles with these primitive half-formed feathers probably lived in the previous or Triassic Period. After you have learned how to read the record in the rocks, you may explore some Triassic rocks and find this early bird.

The most ancient bird-reptile that has ever been discovered was found in the Jurassic rocks of Germany. His name is Archaeopteryx. He was mostly covered with fine feathers (Figure 13-1), but his head had few feathers and showed his reptilian ancestry. He was a feeble flier.

The Archaeopteryx, who met with an untimely death by falling into the mud and who thereby preserved his skeleton and feathers for our inspection, still retained some very reptilian habits. He ate little animals as his ancestors had done when they used to jump from the branches of the trees. He still kept his teeth, as you can see by examining his picture, and his head was more scaly than it was feathery. Also, he kept his claws on his front legs or wings, as they are now called. He could in this way cling to the branches of trees as you can see from his picture. Archaeopteryx didn't sing like a song sparrow; his voice was probably harsh and made a sound more like croaking than like singing. You may wonder how we can know anything about his voice, for certainly a fossil doesn't speak, and a voice cannot be caught in the mud and turned into stone. Now Mr. Beebe has described a bird living in South America today that seems a bit primitive, although certainly is not related to Archaeopteryx. His name is hoatzin (Figure 13-3), and his voice is more like that of a reptile than that of a bird. So it is that we guess, but only guess, and this is always dangerous, that the voice of Archaeopteryx may have been a croak.

Figure 13-1. Archaeopteryx — fossil below and restoration above. This primitive "bird," really a reptile-bird, was probably a meat eater and ate small animals and insects more often than fruit.

(American Museum of Natural History)

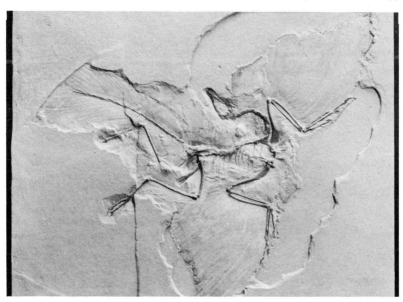

Figure 13-2.   This is a very interesting restoration. Here you see reptiles that were not birds (the pterodactyl) and Archaeopteryx (a "bird," neither reptile nor bird). Do you recognize Archaeopteryx?

(American Museum of Natural History)

In a very entertaining book, *Animals of the Past,* by F. A. Lucas, we read: "Mr. Quelch, who has studied these curious birds in their native wilds of British Guiana, tells us that soon after hatching, the nestlings begin to crawl about by means of their legs and wings, the well-developed claws [on their wings] being constantly in use for hooking to surrounding objects. If they are drawn from the nest by means of their legs, they hold on firmly to the twigs, both with their bill and wings; and if the nest be upset they hold on to all objects with which they come in contact by bill, feet, and wings, making considerable use of the bill with the help of the clawed wings, to raise themselves to a higher level."

In the next period the descendants of Archaeopteryx lost their teeth and the claws on their wings, and became more like modern birds. But there were also rivals of Archaeopteryxs. These rivals of the birds were their cousins and are called pterodactyls or "wing-fingers" (Figure 13-4). In the next period, called the Cretaceous, the pterodactyls grew so large that they were twenty feet from tip to tip of their outspread wings. They were the largest creatures that ever learned how to fly and were more like bats than like birds, for they had neither scales nor feathers. Their wings were enormous sheets of skin, and in order to be light, the bones were hollow and filled with air. But while they looked like bats,

Figure 13-3.   The hoatzin. Why do some call him a primitive bird? Don't confuse him with Archaeopteryx. *(American Museum of Natural History)*

they were neither bats nor the ancestors of bats, for bats are mammals and are descended from primitive mammals, which at this time were running for their lives from dinosaurs, from birds with teeth, and from these same "flying dragons."

Perhaps the pterodactyl always started his flight by jumping from a cliff just as his ancestors had done when they used to jump from a tree. Then he probably soared like a hawk. In this he was very skillful, for there is reason to believe that in the next period he used to start from the chalk cliffs of Kan-

Figure 13-4.   A pterodactyl with the full splendor of his wings — which are enormous sheets of skin.   *(American Museum of Natural History)*

sas and soar for hundreds of miles over the shallow sea that covered a part of the great western plains in those days of the remote Cretaceous Period.

The greatest of all pterodactyls is called Pteranodon, a creature whose spread of wings measured twenty feet. He was carefully studied by S. P. Langley, Secretary of the Smithsonian Institution at Washington, when he was devising one of the first flying-machines, for Pteranodon was one of the most perfect flying devices that the fauna of the earth had ever created.

In *Flying Reptiles,* W. D. Matthew says that Pteranodon was "a marvelously elaborate mechanism, gigantic in size, perfected in every detail of adaptation to its singular mode of life, automatic and precise in its response to every gust of the changing wind, to every distant flicker of light or shade that might indicate some prospect of prey or warn of lurking enemy. I can see him soaring as the great sea birds do today, sweeping tirelessly across the broad glittering surface of the Cretaceous seas, patrolling them from dawn to dark in search of such unwary fish . . . as might be sunning themselves at the surface and come within reach of the sudden swoop from above. . . . At night he would perhaps return to the shore many, many miles distant and hang himself upon some favored roost — tree or rocky point — anywhere that would be securely out of reach of the dinosaurs and other fierce reptilian beasts of prey which lived upon the land."

Just how a pterodactyl walked is a puzzling problem. Perhaps they just folded their wings and walked away. Some had long tails like Dimorphodon. When Dimorphodon was in a hurry, he looked something like an old-fashioned cavalry officer with spurs and long saber and a fierce expression.

One of the best fossil pterodactyls can be seen at the Peabody Museum of Yale University, and another fossil skeleton is on exhibit at the American Museum of Natural History of New York City.

The Jurassic must have been an interesting period for the dinosaurs and primitive mammals.

It was a flying time — this middle period in the Age of Reptiles. Maybe encouraged by the example of the reptiles, some insects began to fly. The mosquito appeared (Figure 13-5), and he has been a nuisance ever since he developed wings.

Bees, flies, and butterflies appeared in this flying period. Gradually the forest was beginning to be filled with insect life, including bright-colored butterflies. In the next period we will see how the flowers spread over the land and, with the birds and insects, made the world look modern.

During the Jurassic Period the air was warm, and deep forests grew in Greenland, for then that name would have been appropriate. During most of the time the land was quiet so that the dinosaurs were not shaken by earthquakes and were not frightened by rivers of lava from bursting volcanoes. However, toward the close of the period great changes took place on the Pacific Coast of North America. As in the Triassic Period, numbers of volcanoes, from California to Alaska, spouted lava. In addition, the hot interior of the earth seemed to get restless and boiled up through the crust, pushing the rocks and their fossils high into the air; some of these blocks of rock were hundreds of miles long, and when one edge was very much more elevated than the other, some of our grandest mountains were formed. Much later (really at the end of the Cretaceous), there came the beginnings of the Sierra Nevada Mountains, the Coast Range, and the Cascade Mountains. Between the Sierra Nevada Mountains and the Coast Range a valley was formed, and we now call this land the Great Valley of California.

At the same time the land where the Rocky Mountains now stand sank, forming a long, narrow depression. Such a depression in the crust of the earth usually precedes the formation of a great chain of mountains. And it did here again, and the mountains formed on what is now our Western Coast. The hot melted rock below the surface of the earth came up quickly.

Figure 13-5.   When giant dinosaurs roamed over the land, these huge mosquitoes also flourished. They are not the direct ancestors of our own mosquitoes, but they are their cousins, who lived in what is now called the Gobi Desert in Asia. These fossils were found by the expedition of the American Museum of Natural History.

(American Museum of Natural History)

It came up so quickly when the Coast Range and Sierra Nevada Mountains rose that many small cracks were formed in the land as it was pushed up. Some of these cracks were filled with a melted white rock called quartz. You have probably seen quartz crystals in museums. This white-hot melted quartz carried with it a very valuable and rare metal — gold. During the millions of years that followed, the surfaces of these mountains crumbled into rocks and dust, for you remember that the O_2 in the air is always attaching itself to the rocks and making them crumble. Then rain came and washed all the pieces down into the valley. This quartz containing the small particles of gold crumbled with the rest of the rock and was washed down the sides of the mountains by streams and rain. In this way some of the quartz became ground into very fine dust and the little particles of gold were set free. In 1849 a man found that some of the soil in this Great Valley of California was full of these little free particles of gold. Since then, many millions of dollars' worth of gold have been taken from the California ground. Some of this very hot melted rock that was forced through the cracks of the earth at this time contained copper and silver as well as gold.

The poor little descendants of Dromatherium of Virginia continued to have a hard time, for the mammals were still so small and timid that "none could look a dinosaur in the face," according to Professor Schuchert of Yale.

In the next period these great dinosaurs became extinct, and the little mammals in their turn grew large and began to rule the world.

14

The Cretaceous Period

We have now come to the last and a very long period in the Age of Reptiles, the Cretaceous Period. It began about 135 million years ago and lasted for perhaps 60 million years.

During most of this time the air was warm. In Greenland and Alaska there were forests of cinnamon trees, fig trees, tree ferns, laurel, and many other plants that are now found only far south of the Arctic Ocean. It was so warm that there was no cold weather even in Greenland. During half the year the nights there were long and dark just as they are today; but the air was so warm and moist that the trees grew through all the year. No man was there to watch them grow, and the armored dinosaurs and flying dragons made no records of it. However, the trees themselves made a record; and we can read that record in the fossil tree trunks we find in Greenland and Alaska.

When you cut down a tree or saw its trunk in two, you will find a large number of rings marked in the wood. They will start with a very small ring in the center and end with a large ring just inside of the bark (Figure 14-1). If the tree was just eight years old when it was cut down, you will be able to count eight rings, for a new ring is grown each year.

Figure 14-1.   This huge tree trunk also tells you its age. Each ring is one year's growth. About how old is the tree?

(United States Plywood Corporation Photo)

When you find the stump of a large tree, you can always tell how old it is by counting the number of rings. These rings are made because the tree grows only in summer. Each winter the tree stops growing or grows only a very little, and each summer it adds a new layer of wood around the old growth. If it were summer all the time and the air were moist and warm all through the year, the tree would grow a little every day. Then the rings would be very indistinct and you would have to have bright eyes to see them. If the tree became a fossil, these faint rings would disappear. So when we find fossils of large trees in Greenland and Alaska and cannot find any rings of growth, we know that they grew all through the year and that the air was moist and warm in winter as well as in summer. Some day you may study rings of growth in the great redwood and sequoia trees of the Pacific Coast. Then you will be able to tell the years in the history of North America that were rainy, when the trees grew rapidly, and those that were dry when the trees grew slowly; for when the tree has plenty of water to drink, it grows well and adds that year a thick ring of wood, but when there is a dry year and the tree is thirsty most of the time, it grows very slowly and adds only a very thin ring of wood to its trunk.

While the trees were flourishing, it was a very bad period for mountains. During those long millions of years the mountains were crumbling and the pieces were being washed down into the valleys until only low hills were left and the ocean spread over the land, forming large, shallow inland seas. On the edges of these seas great swamps and peat bogs were formed, which later became submerged and were baked into the coal that is found all the way from Canada to Arizona. In Colorado alone it is estimated that there are 34,000 million tons of the coal of the Cretaceous Period.

Another thing that we use much as we do coal was made during this period. It is oil, called petroleum, from which gasoline and kerosene are made. When a little shellfish dies, tiny globules of oil that were in its body escape to the water, for all fishes, you know, are very oily. If the water is clear, these small globules of oil rise to the surface, where they are lost and gradually disappear. On the other hand, if the water is muddy and not too much disturbed by swift current, these tiny globules attach themselves to the little particles of mud, for the globules of oil and the particles of mud are very friendly and always get together if they can. After a while the mud settles to the bottom of the shallow sea and carries its little oil companions with it. Then the mud is sometimes buried deep in the earth and is compressed into rock. We dig wells in this rock and pump out the oil. In Wyoming and Texas, and especially in Mexico, we get much oil from rock made out of the mud of the Cretaceous Period. From one well in Mexico 40 million barrels of oil were taken in five years.

During most of this period of low, well-rounded hills and many shallow seas and swamps, the Mississippi River did not flow into the Gulf of Mexico but across the Great Plains into the Pacific Ocean. It probably flowed through Arkansas. It was a long journey in those days for the little drop of water that joined the Ohio River near where Pittsburgh is now and slowly flowed down the rivers and across the broad Mississippi Valley and the plains of Arkansas, Texas, New Mexico, and Arizona. Finally, it joined the great Pacific Ocean. During this journey that drop of water would have seen some' of the most remarkable animals that ever lived on the earth.

You remember that way back in the Triassic Period the reptiles had broken up into groups that became so different from each other that some lived on the banks of shallow seas and ate leaves and plants, and some lived in the forests and ate the animals that they could catch.

These meat eaters became in this Cretaceous Period the most powerful and ferocious land animals that have ever lived. They came from a long line of many generations of reptiles, which stemmed from the Triassic Period. During the Jurassic and Cretaceous Periods the descendants of these reptiles became bigger, swifter, and more cruel, until they ruled all the forests and plains and shores. The giant king of the tyrant lizards is called *Tyrannosaurus rex*. In the American Museum of Natural History you can see a magnificent skeleton of this king lizard (Figure 14-2). *Tyrannosaurus rex* was so tall that he could have seized a pterdoctyl from the top of an ordinary telephone pole. The old tyrant didn't eat vege-

Figure 14-2.   The giant king of the tyrant lizards, *Tyrannosaurus rex*. At
the right one of his relatives, Triceratops. After a painting by C. R. Knight.
(American Museum of Natural History)

tables with his meat, but he did eat those cousins of his whose
only food was vegetables.

These peaceful cousins developed some very strong armored skin, which served as protection against the meat
eaters. Of course you will at once say that this dinosaur
armorplate came into existence from purely natural causes,
because only those with hard skin ever survived. After millions of years some survivors became like little walking forts.
Some are called Triceratops (Figure 14-3), because they had
three horns on their heads, and *tri* means three.

Figure 14-3.   Triceratops, a member of the dinosaur family, Ceratopsia; he was often attacked by the savage *Tyrannosaurus rex*. After a model by C. R. Knight at the American Museum of Natural History.

(American Museum of Natural History)

Another dinosaur, Stegosaurus, carried his protection around with him (Figures 14-4 and 14-5). He was well protected, but the bony part of his head that held his brain was extremely small.

One group of peaceful leaf-eating dinosaurs grew to an enormous size. They were the largest animals that ever walked on land. One was Diplodocus and another was Brontosaurus (Figure 14-6). Imagine Brontosaurus in a field today, 16 feet high, 70 feet long, and weighing 70,000 pounds. He weighed as much as five African elephants. It must have been hard work for his mouth to eat enough leaves to keep his stomach from being always hungry, for it is believed he had to eat 700 pounds of leaves a day to keep from starving. Some of these reptiles lived in the Triassic. Plateosaurus (Figure 12-7), whom you have met before when you traveled through the Triassic Period, was a prominent leaf eater in that earlier time. Even in those ancient days Plateosaurus had

Figure 14-4.   The dinosaur, Stegosaurus. From a painting by C. R. Knight.
(© Chicago Natural History Museum)

Figure 14-5.   A skeleton of Stegosaurus; he was certainly well protected.
(American Museum of Natural History)

Figure 14-6. Huge and terrifying? Yet Brontosaurus was a vegetarian. After a painting by C. R. Knight. *(American Museum of Natural History)*

been eating his meals from the neighboring bushes for so many generations that he had developed rather large and clumsy feet. You remember he didn't have to run to catch a bush, for the bush always stood very still and let him walk up slowly and eat it. Therefore, he didn't need spry little feet for running and jumping, but he did need large, round feet so that he could stand for hours and eat the leaves from a tree or wade in marshy places without being mired. You notice Brontosaurus and Diplodocus had feet that were very good to stand on but not so good for running. Sauropods is the name given to these giant leaf-eating dinosaurs with "elephant" feet.

The sauropods had good reason not to be friendly with their cousins the meat eaters; the American Museum of

Natural History has found the skeletons of two dinosaurs that had been overwhelmed by some accident while one was eating the other.

The meat-eating dinosaurs seemed always to be fighting each other. A scene such as that in Figure 14-7 was quite common; here one Dryptosaurus is fighting another to the death.

In the Triassic Period you will remember that a family of reptiles made their living by catching fish in the sea. Their group name is Ichthyosaurus. The portrait of an early member of the group is given in Figure 12-5, and his name is Cymbospondylus. He belonged to one of the old reptile families

Figure 14-7.   No vegetarians these. Dryptosaurus always seemed to be attacking other dinosaurs — for his dinner, no doubt. After a painting by C. R. Knight.   *(American Museum of Natural History)*

who had become fishermen. In the Cretaceous Period this family became very numerous and very powerful. In Figure 14-8, a mother ichthyosaur, perhaps twenty-five feet long, is seen followed by her family.

Those who lived in the seas of Kansas in the Cretaceous times must have been ever dreading the mosasaurs. In the Cretaceous Period, the mosasaurs were probably rulers of the seas, just as *Tyrannosaurus rex* had become the ruler of the land. The head of the family in Cretaceous times was named Tylosaurus. His headquarters were in the shallow seas that covered a large part of Kansas. There he caught large fish (Figure 14-9), and his descendants became so numerous that bones of a thousand mosasaurs have been taken from the chalk cliffs of Kansas. This ruler of the Cretaceous seas was sometimes forty-five feet long and more dangerous than are the man-eating crocodiles of India.

The ichthyosaurs and mosasaurs had rivals, the plesiosaurs. We read about plesiosaurs in the Triassic Period (Figure 12-4), and now in the Jurassic and Cretaceous Periods we find them fighting for their share of the food in all the shallow seas. The plesiosaur has been described by F. A. Lucas as "a snake threaded through the body of a turtle." This was how he looked, but of course he had no shell. During this, the last period in the life of plesiosaurs, some grew to be forty-five feet long.

In the Triassic Period we found that some other reptiles had adopted the seafaring life. These were the chelonians or turtles. Placochelys (Figure 12-3) was a distinguished ancestor of this family. The chelonians, however, followed the fashions of the Cretaceous Period, and grew large. The giant sea

Figure 14-8.   An Ichthyosaurus, some 20-25 feet long, on the hunt for fish. After a painting by C. R. Knight.

(American Museum of Natural History)

Figure 14-9.   A giant mosasaur from the inland Cretaceous seas of Kansas chasing the fish named Portheus. After a drawing by C. R. Knight at the American Museum of Natural History.

(American Museum of Natural History)

turtle Archelon (Figure 14-10) illustrates how well the chelonians imitated the other giants of the Cretaceous Period.

Even one of the birds grew large in this giant period. His name is Hesperornis (Figure 14-11), the great toothed diver. Notice he had no wings at all.

And what was the situation like on land in the late Cretaceous? Possibly the landscape looked somewhat like that in Figure 14-12. No, man was not yet on the scene.

In these warm, shallow seas during the Cretaceous Period there grew millions upon millions of tiny animals called Foraminifera (Figure 14-13). Each animal had a shell that was no larger than a grain of sand; so you can see how many,

Figure 14-10.   The giant sea turtle Archelon.
(American Museum of Natural History)

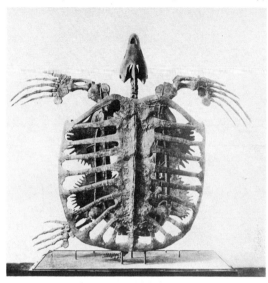

Figure 14-11.   The great toothed diver, Hesperornis. Covered with smooth, soft feathers, this bird caught fishes by diving, but he lost the art of flying. After a drawing by J. M. Gleeson at the American Museum of Natural History.   *(American Museum of Natural History)*

Figure 14-12.   A scene in the late Cretaceous. At the right is a dinosaur, Edmontosaurus. The ostrich-like dinosaur (not an ostrich, of course) in the background is Struthiomimus.   (© *Chicago Natural History Museum*)

many times the shells in the picture have been magnified. When the tiny animal is alive, he floats through the water and is often eaten in large numbers by the small fish. When the Foraminifera escape being eaten alive and die a natural death, their shells drop to the bottom of the sea. The bottom of the ocean is full of tiny shells of all kinds. Apparently the warm, moist air and the quiet, clear, and shallow seas of the Cretaceous Period made these little Foraminifera very nu-

merous, and instead of growing to be giants like many of the
other fauna and flora, they simply grew great in numbers,
piling their shells in heaps on the bottom of the seas. In the
course of ages these masses of tiny shells became hardened,
and now we call them chalk. The Romans called chalk *creta,*
and so much chalk was made at this time that we call the
period Cretaceous. You are probably wondering why we
don't find oil in these masses of chalk. You remember that
the little animals, in order to leave oil in the rock, must die
in muddy water, so that the tiny globules of oil could unite
with particles of mud and settle to the bottom. Where these

Foraminifera lived, the water was clear and the little globules of oil were washed away, so that only pure white shells accumulated at the bottom of the sea.

This period so marvelous for the development of the flora and fauna finally came to a terrible end. The crust of the earth, which had been quiet for so many millions of years, began to wrinkle. For most of the Cretaceous Period a long, narrow sea had covered the land that is now occupied by the Rocky Mountains from Alaska to Mexico. Where the Andes now are in South America there was a corresponding narrow sea. In the Jurassic Period we found the land was sinking in a narrow valley from Alaska to Mexico. You remember that we then suspected that this valley would make a weak point in the crust and that if ever the earth wrinkled again, huge mountains might rise where this valley had been. And so they did at the end of the Cretaceous Period.

Figure 14-13. These shells of tiny animals fairly heaped the bottom of the oceans — only to form chalk cliffs. But the living substance of a number of them was changed to oil.   *(American Museum of Natural History)*

Due to the slow wrinkling of the crust of the earth, the long, narrow sea extending from Alaska to Mexico began to grow very shallow. As the ground rose here and there, the sea was cut off from the ocean. Then the bottom rose so that much dry land appeared and only lakes were left. Finally even these lakes disappeared. The land kept on rising for millions of years until finally the great Rocky Mountains stood where once Tylosaurus had ruled the sea. At the same time the Andes Mountains of South America were formed.

Before this happened, the Mississippi River flowed westward, perhaps over the land that is now called Arkansas, to the Pacific Ocean. When the Rocky Mountains rose, the old river channel was blocked, so that the water had to find a new outlet to the sea. Fortunately, at the same time the land now called Louisiana and Mississippi sank a little and allowed the river to cut a channel to the Gulf of Mexico. Ever since then the great Mississippi Valley has sent all its waters to the Atlantic Ocean by way of the Gulf of Mexico. As the Mississippi River dug its channel deep down in the rock, it flowed through canyons with sides like cliffs. This was millions of years ago, and now the cliffs have been nearly all worn away so that the river often overflows its banks.

Toward the end of the Cretaceous Period and the beginning of the next period, the Eocene, the Appalachian Mountains, which had sunk once, had risen again. On both the Atlantic and Pacific Coasts the land extended into the ocean much farther than it does now. Florida was very wide and was connected with Cuba.

With the growth of the mighty Rocky Mountains and the new growth of the old Appalachian Mountains, the air became so cold that there was a huge glacier in the southwestern part of Colorado. The inland seas and lakes were all dried up and drained by rivers that flowed through steep banks to the sea. As the inland seas disappeared and the moist warm air grew cold, the huge animals died. Scientists are not sure why they died out; here is one of the great mysteries of science. Even if they could have endured the ice and snow of winter, they would have starved to death, for food in the environment in which they were accustomed to live was becoming scarce. Little by little as the winters grew colder, the giant dinosaurs and the great pterodactyls perished. But although the dinosaurs died out, some reptiles survived. Look around you and note the snakes, lizards, turtles, crocodiles, and their relatives — remnants of a proud group.

15

The Eocene Period

We have been on a long journey down through the ages. We have watched our animals develop and successfully survive one crisis after another. Now we enter on a new group of periods. They are the last in this history, for we are approaching the end of our story. In this group of periods the great apes appear and man finally emerges as a branch of the order called primates. There are five of these geological periods, which are short in time compared with many other periods, but of momentous value to us. We speak of them all as "recent," and the first one is called "Dawn of the Recent," or in Greek, Eocene. It began perhaps 60 million years ago and lasted about 20 million years.

If you had really taken this imaginary journey, if you had been blindfolded at the end of the Cretaceous Period and had been allowed to look around you for the first time when the Eocene Period was well advanced, you would have been amazed at the change of scene — a new and almost modern world would have met you at every turn.

"The passage of time from the Cretaceous to the succeeding Eocene is shrouded in darkness; and the 'new dawn' follows a long night. It is as if the lights in a playhouse had been abruptly extinguished, and after a lapse had been restored, disclosing a stage crowded with new characters.

"The transition times were doubtless of long duration, and full of stirring events; but their archives for the most part have either been destroyed, or have yet to be discovered. The results, however, of what then took place are plain enough. There had been a great elimination of old forms of reptile and other life; and mammals had become dominant. Dinosaurs, herbivorous and carnivorous, had one and all vanished from the scene — iguanadonts . . . , stegosaurs with their battlemented backs and the rest of the fraternity. Old Triceratops with his thrice-horned head, and Elizabethan frill, seems to have held out as long as any; but fortune failed him at last. In short the old reptile nobility, unable to march with the times, had been swept away. Nor had ichthyosaurs, plesiosaurs, mosasaurs, and flying lizards fared any better. They had all quitted the stage never to return." So writes H. R. Knipe in his book, *Evolution in the Past*.

While we know very little about the early part of the Eocene Period, we do know that the many mammals that now appear must have been developing during the latter part of the Cretaceous, for their fossil remains have been found. Perhaps it was due to the disappearance of the large reptiles that the small mammals "which couldn't look a reptile in the face" developed into goodly sized animals of a number of varieties, which ultimately became our familiar horses, bears, rats, cows, lions, apes, and even men.

North America must have been a beautiful country during this Dawn of the Recent. The mountains along the Pacific Coast were worn into rounded hills. The rushing torrents with rapids and waterfalls had disappeared. To be sure, there were many volcanoes in the states of Oregon and Washington, but for the most part North America was at peace with the interior of the earth, and volcanic eruptions and earthquakes were rare. The great Appalachian Mountains were now beginning to crumble away, and before the end of the period they had become gracefully curved low hills, covered with forests and green food for the new mammals.

The great rivers that we know so well were not far from their present locations. The Colorado, Snake, and Columbia Rivers of the West Coast drained their countries of the surplus rainfall much as they do today. In the East there was the St. Lawrence River, which flowed over land that has now sunk below the Atlantic Ocean, for the land through which the river flowed was more than one thousand feet higher above the ocean than at present. There was dry land where the fishermen now catch codfish on the Grand Banks. You can even now see where this ancient St. Lawrence River flowed by looking at the maps that give the depths of the ocean for the region just south of Newfoundland. The Connecticut and Hudson Rivers flowed through valleys that closely resemble their channels of today, except that the mouths of these rivers were at points that are now far out to sea, for since this period the land has sunk and allowed the ocean to flood a portion of these ancient river channels. The Hudson River flowed through a deep canyon and reached the sea at a place now under several hundred feet of water.

We found that during the last period the land now occupied by Mississippi and Louisiana had sunk enough to enable the Mississippi River to cut a new channel between deep canyon walls to the Gulf of Mexico. During the Eocene Period the sinking of the southern part of the Mississippi Valley continued until the Gulf of Mexico flowed over this sunken land as far north as where the Ohio River now flows into the Mississippi River. Then for some unknown reason the land began to rise again until now the Mississippi River flows into the Gulf of Mexico much as it did at the end of the Cretaceous Period.

If a Californian had wandered through the Eocene woodlands, he would have felt very much at home, for the great sequoia trees made stately forests in Canada as well as in the country now occupied by the Rocky Mountains. These wonderful trees — sometimes over three hundred feet high and fifteen to twenty feet in diameter — live to be several thousand years old. "I never saw a 'big tree' that had died a natural death; barring accidents they seem to be immortal, being exempt from all the diseases that afflict and kill other trees. Unless destroyed by man, they live on indefinitely until burned, smashed by lightning or cast down by storms or by the giving way of the ground on which they stand." John Muir is thus quoted by C. Schuchert in *Historical Geology*. In the Eocene Period they grew from Spitzbergen within the Arctic Circle to the middle of Italy. They grew in China as well as over most of North America. They are among the few great giants of the past living today. Perhaps they are the biggest living things that have grown on the earth. California is their guardian, for there only have they survived.

A curious feature of those days was the unusual variety of trees that grew in the same forest. Nowadays an oak tree will grow only where the air is cold enough to kill a banana tree. Yet oak, banana, fig, and breadfruit trees grew side by side on the coast of North America. Now the breadfruit tree is found only in the tropics.

The world had fewer bleak and ice-cold countries in those Eocene days. Magnolia trees and delicate ferns grew along the Yukon River in Alaska. In Greenland there were forests of cypress trees like those now found in the swamps of the southern states, cedars, sycamores, magnolias, willows, poplars, bayberries, elm trees, tulip trees, oaks, maples, birches, ash, hazelnut trees, sequoias, sumacs, plum trees, persimmon trees, and grapevines. The shores of the country we now call southern England were full of crocodiles and huge water snakes, and forests of palm trees flourished on the land. Birds with bills notched like a saw flew over the Thames River where London has since been built.

In Eocene days the Mississippi River was a northern stream, for its mouth was near St. Louis, where now we have snow in winter. However, this Eocene Mississippi River had dense tropical foliage on its banks the year round (Figure 15-1).

Figure 15-1. The Eocene Mississippi had dense foliage on its banks, a kind of tropical foliage, which may have resembled this scene of Nipa palms growing along a river in the Philippines.
(Magno G. Matela, Dept. of General Services, Republic of the Philippines)

For the first time the flora had begun to show color on a large scale, for the flowering plants now predominated in the plains and forests. Heretofore, ferns, evergreens, and those queer Carboniferous trees had been the prevailing flora.

Probably also the birds had brilliant plumage in this period, for the primitive ancestors of many of our well-known birds lived during the approximate 20 million years of the Dawn of the Recent. Here is a list of a few of the birds that can trace their family tree back to the Eocene: albatross, goose, crane, flamingo, stork, owl, woodpecker, swift, quail, nuthatch, starling, lark, and warbler.

One remarkable bird was Diatryma (Figure 15-2). The Diatryma in this dawn period grew huge and muscular. Like Hesperornis (Figure 14-11) in the Cretaceous Period, he had lost the art of flying. He stalked through the forests and over

Figure 15-2.   Diatryma, a giant Eocene bird of North America. From a drawing by E. S. Christman at the American Museum of Natural History.
(American Museum of Natural History)

the plains of North America, killing and eating small animals. The Diatryma did not adapt, however, and some of the animals of that period grew swift and savage as tigers and began eating Diatryma until finally Diatryma existed no more.

Through this veritable Garden of Eden, the primitive mammals now roamed almost without fear, for their chief enemies, the giant reptiles, had perished. Perhaps only Diatryma was dangerous, and he was rare. To be sure, there were alligators and large water snakes, and the ocean was full of sharks; but why should primitive mammals fear these water creatures as they ran through the forests of tall sequoias and oaks and perhaps rested in the shade of a four-foot palm leaf? They prospered greatly and grew and multiplied. We call them primitive mammals because they were early mammals and unspecialized ones. They are members of the stock from which the carnivores and hoofed mammals arose. They were neither dog, horse, cat, nor elephant. They were just archaic mammals and in some ways resembled all those animals of which they are the common ancestor.

Although this wonderful Eocene world was theirs and although there was hardly an enemy to disturb their slumbers, yet the archaic mammals began killing and eating each other as the great reptiles had done before them. These early meat eaters are called creodonts. Patriofelis was a prominent member of this group (Figure 15-3).

Some of the archaic mammals developed a taste for plants and leaves instead of insects and fruit. They were a peaceful crowd, which would rather run than fight. Phenocodus (Figure 15-4) was one of these early hoofed plant eaters.

Eohippus was the first primitive horse — no larger than a small dog. Dawn-horse he is sometimes called, for that is the meaning of the Greek word eohippus (Figure 15-5). The familiar hoof is missing, for in those Eocene days he ran on four

Figure 15-3.   Patriofelis. He wants that alligator, but he doesn't dare go into the water after him. From a painting by C. R. Knight under the direction of H. F. Osborn of the American Museum of Natural History.

(American Museum of Natural History)

Figure 15-4.   Would the horse of today recognize his early Eocene ancestor? Phenocodus' family name was Condylarth, and some of his descendants became rhinoceroses. After a painting by C. R. Knight under the direction of H. F. Osborn at the American Museum of Natural History.

(American Museum of Natural History)

toes on the front feet and three toes on the hind ones. Those of the little dawn-horses that were slow couldn't compete in the struggle for survival (Figure 15-6). Only those horses survived that could run like mad and escape the rapidly developing meat eaters. The faster the plant eaters ran, the quicker, it seemed, the meat eaters developed and adapted themselves to hunting their prey. So the contest continued for millions of years, as it has been doing in the world of fauna ever since one group of cells declared war on another and ate

Figure 15-5.   Eohippus, the dawn-horse of the early part of the Eocene. After a drawing by C. R. Knight at the American Museum of Natural History.   (*American Museum of Natural History*)

them alive. The slow and weak perished miserably, and from these bloody scenes emerged the swift horse and the savage tiger of our own day.

We have already found that early in the Eocene, the little dawn-horse Eohippus was scampering through the forests. As his descendants developed and became adapted to the changing environment, his middle toe grew larger and the other four toes grew smaller. Gradually the other toes vanished and the one big center toe took their place. We now call this big toe the horse's hoof. In Figure 15-7 you can follow this change in the skeleton of the foot through the various ages to the present time.

As we have already found, there are often several reasons

Figure 15-6.   The grim result of a struggle for existence. This dawn-horse was too slow. After a painting by C. R. Knight, made under the direction of H. F. Osborn for the American Museum of Natural History.

(American Museum of Natural History)

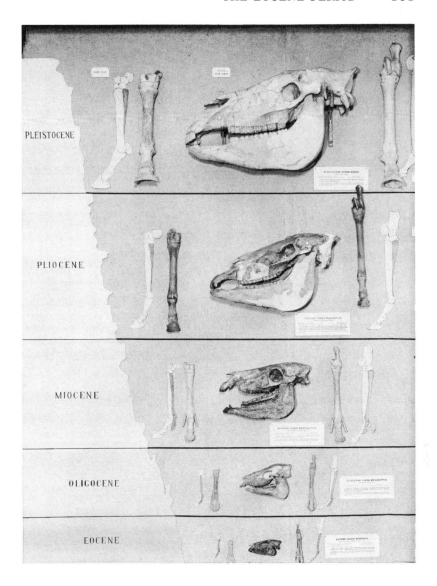

Figure 15-7. Follow the story of the evolution of the horse from these pictures. How did the hoof develop? How did the skull develop? The Eocene horse was, of course, the ancestor of the others.

(American Museum of Natural History)

why certain events have taken place, and the change in the shape of the horse's foot may be another example. We shall find later that in subsequent periods the air grew colder and many of the forests became grassy plains. In any event, the horse developed into the animal you know and whose skeleton you see in Figure 15-8. Trace the development of the horse from Eohippus on the left in Figure 15-8 to our modern horse, Equus, on the right.

When food is abundant, animals grow larger. The larger

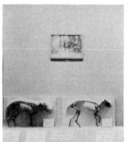

Figure 15-8.   After 50 million years the descendant of the little Eohippus on the left of the line has become the magnificent horse of today at the right of the line. Now the gasoline engine is taking the horse's place. So evolution (in terms of a change of the environment) may be as relentless for the horse as it was for the dinosaur.

(American Museum of Natural History)

animals have some advantage, for their size may help them protect themselves better than can their smaller companions. The horse was no exception to this rule. On the plains he found plenty of food, and for tens of millions of years he grew steadily larger and swifter.

Even before the Eocene Period had closed, this dawn-horse had made progress and gave promise of his future greatness. Orohippus is the name of the horse that represents this second stage.

During all this time one branch of the primitive mammals continued to live on fruit and insects. Like the early mammals in the Triassic Period, these mammals were small and spent most of their time in the trees. They were early members of our branch of the animal world, for they were primitive primates. Notharctus of Wyoming (Figure 15-9) is often regarded as the leading North American member of this group. It is difficult to trace any family likeness, for he does not look much like any man we ever saw. Yet he must have been a bright little animal during those Eocene years, for some of the descendants of his generation became the rulers of the earth.

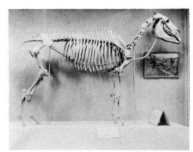

Figure 15-9. A member of one of the "first families" of Wyoming in the Eocene days. From some of his remote cousins we are probably descended. Notharctus was perhaps a yard long if we include his tail.

(American Museum of Natural History)

Over millions of years the primate's face was changed; the snout became smaller and the eyes took on a more prominent place.

Some little primates got as far as this first change in their faces, and then they stopped developing. We have met with this curious thing ever since we began to explore the ancient periods of this earth. Now we find in the East Indies a little tree-living mammal that has changed little from the time when his Eocene ancestors began to develop their eyes and to ignore their noses. His name is Tarsius (Figure 15-10).

Although you may think you are seeing a family likeness, we must emphasize that we are not descended from Tarsius. Apparently the tarsiers gave rise only to more tarsiers.

Figure 15-10.   Tarsius lives in the East Indies and still closely resembles his Eocene ancestor. He looks like a relative of ours, but we are not descended from his line.   (N.Y. *Zoological Society Photo*)

16

The Oligocene Period

In order that we may understand the names that have been given to the remaining four periods in the earth's history, let us learn them all now so that, by arranging them in their proper sequence, we can find their true meaning. The latest period, the one from which we are now emerging, is called the "Most Recent" or Pleistocene. It began about one million years ago. Previous to Pleistocene came Pliocene ("More Recent"), which commenced about ten million years ago and lasted about nine million years. Then as we go back in time we come to the "Less Recent" or Miocene. The periods are growing longer as they grow more ancient, for the Miocene began perhaps 30 million years ago and lasted for approximately 20 million years.

Finally we come to the Oligocene Period, the subject of this chapter. Translated, the name means "Little of the Recent." It began about 40 million years ago and lasted probably at least 20 million years.

No stirring events marked this period; no large mountain ranges rose to the clouds, no new and strange race of animals appeared, and also no very well-known rulers of the earth disappeared. Life on land and in the sea and air continued to develop during the Oligocene much as it had in the preceding Eocene. You remember that during the Eocene the mountains were crumbling away and the air was growing warm and moist. The Oligocene gave the earth 10 million more years in which to carry on this work, for during the Oligocene the wearing away of the hills continued until the land was almost a plain (peneplain) and not much above the ocean.

In outline, North America began to have a more modern appearance. Greenland began to separate from Canada, but the East Coast was still as far out to sea as it was in the Eocene. That rising of the land in the lower Mississippi Valley continued so that by the middle of the Oligocene Period the great river flowed into the Gulf of Mexico at a point not far from the northern boundary of Louisiana. Florida was merely a small island, for nearly all of that peninsula was under water as well as the southern parts of Alabama, Mississippi, and Georgia. The West Indies, which in the Eocene had consisted of one extensive island, had disappeared entirely beneath the waves. So also had Yucatan, and Panama, if it had existed, would not have needed a canal, for North and South America were widely separated during this period. The sharks, the only cruising submarines in those days, freely swam from ocean to ocean.

On the West Coast, where the entrance to the Gulf of California now lies, the land had begun to sink and to be slowly, very slowly, flooded by the sea. Thus that gulf, so clearly shown in our geographies, began to take its present shape in the Oligocene Period. California had some strange land to its west — a land doomed eventually to sink beneath the sea. The states of Oregon and Washington had a tempestuous prehistoric past, for during the 50 million years of the Oligocene, Miocene, and Pliocene Periods, volcanoes made the night skies lurid and covered the land with ashes and streams of molten lava.

British Columbia, like the eastern coast of North America, extended far into the ocean. Like that land to the west of California, this also sank into the depths of the sea, but so slowly that in the remaining 40 million years of the earth's history it has not entirely disappeared. That coast is full of islands and partly submerged valleys, which are the remnants of its greater past. Finally, we know that Alaska, a little larger than now, was a continuous land bridge between North America and Asia.

The world was like a great greenhouse during the Oligocene Period. Warm, moist air covered the low hills and dense forests (Figure 16-1). When the sun was low in the southern

Figure 16-1.   No cold north winds from Greenland's icy mountains could bring frost to this luxuriant growth, for there existed neither ice nor high mountains to disturb this forest. Nearly all the land in the world was low, with well-rounded hills, and covered with hot moist air.

(American Museum of Natural History)

skies and there were long, dark nights in the north, there must have been tremendous storms that swept over North America from west to east — cyclones of hurricane force. Also this hot air overburdened with little globules of water probably produced thunderstorms of gigantic proportions. Those corridors, one hundred feet high, between the great sequoia trees echoed with the peals of Oligocene thunder and were illuminated with flashes of lightning far surpassing any in our experience.

In these forests and over the plains, in clear weather and in stormy weather, the great age-long contest continued — the survival of the fittest. The meat-eating creodonts were hard pressed, for some rivals that sprang more savagely to the attack had invaded North America. Some of them may have

come from Asia across that land bridge of Alaska. Apparently, many meat eaters had developed more rapidly in Asia, for they treated the creodonts as ruthlessly as the white men from Europe later treated the native Indians. One of the last creodonts to yield to the new supremacy was *Hyaenodon horridus* (Figure 16-2), although he survived for a time in both hemispheres.

The cat family was now supreme; it was the royal family of the sequoia forests. Dinictis (Figure 16-3) was perhaps the first to display modern lines and to develop that athletic jump that has made the family famous. However, he was soon

Figure 16-2.   The huge mammals are Titanotheres. But don't lose sight of Hyaenodon in the lower right. Hyaenodon is apparently the last of his kind; he lived by eating dead animals. This was a poor living, and he lost out in the struggle for existence.   (© *Chicago Natural History Museum*)

surpassed by his cousin Hoplophoneus, who began to display a gleaming pair of ivory teeth that must have been the envy as well as the terror of the Oligocene fauna.

Figure 16-3. It may be that Dinictis represents an intermediate stage between the savage meat-eating creodont and the magnificent and overwhelming saber-toothed tiger. Yet Dinictis survived for some time and was even a contemporary of Hoplophoneus. From a painting by C. R. Knight, under the direction of H. F. Osborn.

(American Museum of Natural History)

While the cats were growing larger and receiving reinforcements from other continents, the horses were adapting even further along the lines of larger bodies and swift flight. You remember that the horse was a peaceful mammal. Mesohippus (Figure 16-4) is the leader of these Oligocene

Figure 16-4.   Mesohippus, a swift light-limbed three-toed horse that lived in North America during the first part of the Oligocene Period. Watching this horse is the primitive tiger Dinictis. After a drawing by C. R. Knight in the American Museum of Natural History.

(American Museum of Natural History)

horses. More and more Mesohippus relied on that middle toe, which slowly developed into a hoof.

Not all the meat eaters had developed into the animals we call the cat family. During the Oligocene Period some descendants of the creodonts developed family traits of their own, but even in the late Eocene they had produced a meat eater that is, perhaps, the earliest representative of the dog family. His name is Cynodictis, and he is often called the ancestor of the fox.

It is a long time now since we have explored the depths of the ocean. Before the Dawn of the Recent it was full of mosasaurs, plesiosaurs, ichthyosaurs, chelonians, and sharks. In the Oligocene, if we had been guests of Neptune, we should have found only two large monsters: whales and sharks.

One of these marine creatures was a mammal that had undertaken a seafaring life. We now call him a whale, and he has been so long in the water that he looks for all the world like a fish. Once upon a time his ancestors ran around on the land, for he is descended from those little primitive mammals that used to hide from dinosaurs in the Jurassic and Cretaceous Periods. Some reptiles took up the fisherman's life and became ichthyosaurs and mosasaurs. Even the great bird Hesperornis (Figure 14-11) gave up flying and earned his living by diving and swimming. Some of the mammals adapted not only to an amphibian's but even a fish's life. The mammal's paws gradually turned into fins in somewhat the same way and for exactly the same reasons that had long before changed the reptile's feet into paddles or finlike structures.

One of the early whales was a queer-looking animal, and he also had a strange name, Zeuglodon (Figure 16-5). In the

Figure 16-5. Zeuglodon, a primitive whale that in the Oligocene Period swam in the water that is now called the Gulf of Mexico. A whaler (and there were no whalers in those days) might wonder whether he were hunting sea serpents or whales. After a drawing by C. R. Knight.

(American Museum of Natural History)

course of time, however, he became more compact and a much faster swimmer. At least, those that didn't change in this way became food for sharks, so that after millions of years the modern whale was developed.

If you had again accepted Neptune's invitation to visit the vast stretches of warm water in the Oligocene, you would have been convinced that the sharks were destined to be undisputed rulers of the sea. They had grown to an unheard-of size, and their ferocity must have been the equal of that of *Tyrannosaurus rex* (Figure 14-2). Charalarodon (Figure 16-6) was the name of this shark, and he was the terror of all that came within the reach of his huge jaws. His family began its career in the Upper Cretaceous and formed probably Nep-

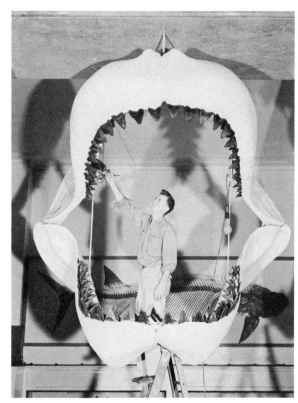

Figure 16-6.   Next to a California sequoia tree, it may be that Charalarodon was the largest living thing that has ever grown upon the earth. As long as a twelve-story building is high, this monster ruled the seas. You may get an idea of his size from his jaws. After a photograph of an exhibit at the American Museum of Natural History.
(American Museum of Natural History)

tune's ablest admirals of the navy until well into the Miocene.

"Once fairly started in life these huge sharks spread themselves throughout the warm seas of the world, for there was none might stand before them and say nay. They swarmed everywhere that the water was sufficiently warm, for their teeth occur in . . . strata in many parts of the world. . . . And then they perished, perished as utterly as did the hosts of Sennacherib. Why? We do not know. Did they devour everything large enough to be eaten . . . and then fall to eating one another? Again we do not know. But perish they did, while the smaller white shark, which came into being at the same time, still lives, as if to emphasize the fact that it is best not to overdo things and that in the long run the victory is not always with the largest," says F. A. Lucas in his delightful little book, *Animals of the Past*.

We have reserved for the last the next stage in our own family history, for we now have before us a fairly good picture of Oligocene geography, climate, and life in forest and sea. For many millions of years the primates lived in this beautiful country of stately forests and brilliant thunderstorms, but amid a turmoil of combat and sudden death. Like Tarsius they continued to live in the trees and to eat fruit and insects. As those early primates swung from branch to branch over the snarling, shrieking death struggle that ever and again occurred far down among the ferns and roots of the tree, they little realized if they looked into the future at all that their descendants were some day to become the rulers of the world.

Life all over the world was much the same as in North America. We have already found that a few of the descendants of the meat-eating Asiatic creodonts had migrated to North America. However, it is the opinion of most students of the subject that for our own family history we must turn to Asia and probably to that part of the country that is now called the Gobi Desert. In those Oligocene days it was covered with a dense forest including many giant sequoias. The tribes of little animals like Notharctus and later the tribe like Tupaia, an animal like Tarsius, were probably there, for these little creatures apparently had spread far and wide.

The primates that looked like Tetonius, an Eocene relative of the living Tarsius, had better eyes than the family of Notharctus, for Notharctus, like many animals, had an eye on each side of his head, very much like a squirrel. After millions of years, however, the primates like Tetonius developed a different kind of face; now they could see the same object with both eyes at the same time. Now in the Oligocene of Egypt was to be found a new kind of primate, called Propliopithecus. After millions of years Propliopithecus had developed a bigger brain than his ancestors who resembled Tarsius.

Although the early primates were a peaceful lot, they must have had at least some differences of opinion in those 10 million Oligocene years, for during that period one group after another left the family of Propliopithecus and started a little tree-living community of their own. As the primate population grew and the trees got crowded, it became even harder to get enough to eat. Then a primate could either move off into a more distant forest and continue to live as his ancestors had done, or he could stay where he was and learn new and better ways of getting food. Probably no primate ever sat on a limb and pondered the choice. As the forests became crowded, each primate every day did the best he could to get his daily food and bring up his family of little primates. Some just naturally wandered farther and farther away, while others developed better ways of getting food and protecting their families and stayed nearer home.

Every group seems to have a limit beyond which it cannot develop. This is true even of individuals. We can learn to run fast, and as we practice more, we run faster; yet try as hard as we may, we never can run as fast as some of our playmates. Some of us can learn arithmetic and geometry, and we have even passed our examination in algebra; but we know in our hearts that we don't understand algebra and that we never will, because our mathematical mind could comprehend no more than geometry. So it seems that all athletes, all mathematicians, and all musicians have a limit beyond which they seem not to be able to go. This is more than a primate characteristic; it is a characteristic of all living things, for it pervades the life of the world.

What would we find happening if we could but appear on the scene of our ancestral beginnings? The pre-monkeys, that is, the ancestors of the monkeys, came perhaps from the tree-dwelling, insect-eating animals that looked much like the living Oriental tree shrew Tupaia. The pre-monkeys include the lemurs on the one hand and our old friend Tarsius on the other. Somewhere and sometime after the Eocene it is thought there were four separate evolutionary lines — the New World monkeys, the Old World monkeys, the apes (from the Oligocene of Egypt), and man. Man, you and I, appear to owe our origin — so present knowledge points — to Australopithecus (Figure 16-7) who appears to have originated during the Pleistocene. So we have a long history. And in the years to come, as more information comes to light, we may have a clearer picture of our earliest ancestor. At present the finger of evidence points to Australopithecus (Figure 16-7), but it seems quite clear that neither Old or New World monkeys led to man.

Figure 16-7.   This is the way a skull of Australopithecus, who may have been our earliest ancestor, appears. There is no doubt that it resembles our skull.   *(American Museum of Natural History)*

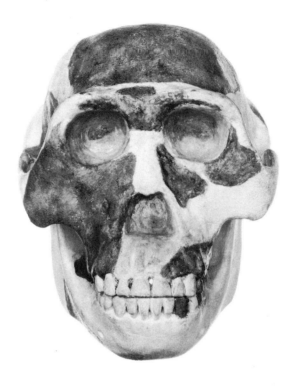

17

The Miocene Period

The Miocene Period, meaning "Less Recent," began about 30 million years ago and lasted perhaps 20 million years. Thus it came down to within a few million years of our own time. When we consider the long spaces of time that we have been using, it would seem as if a period that ended only about seven million years ago might be considered almost historical. However, we must remember that there is a vast difference between a few thousand and a few million years, and a great many very important events took place in the remaining seven million years.

It was during the 20 million years of the Miocene that modern life began to develop the shapes and habits that are familiar to us. One reason for this change was the cooler weather that began toward the end of the period. During a large part of the time, however, that luxuriant greenhouse life continued.

We know a great deal about the trees and insects of the Miocene Age because of those very useful volcanoes. Nothing can be so destructive as a volcano, except perhaps the subsidence of a large section of land beneath the ocean. Yet the volcanoes have preserved for us many interesting things from the past, such as the forests of fossil trees in the Yellowstone National Park and the wonderful ruins of Pompeii. In the Oligocene Period, for instance, the volcanoes did a third convenient thing — they helped preserve an ancient lake called Lake Florissant, and it was done so quickly that thousands of insects and leaves and flowers were caught in the mud, pressed flat, and preserved for us as fossils. Therefore, we suspect that there grew in the western part of the country in the late Oligocene and Miocene such trees and plants as alders, sweet gums, sequoias, and types of hollies (Figure 17-1), as well as oaks, narrow-leafed cottonwoods, pines, wild roses, thistles, asters, sumach, and Virginia creepers. Then there were flora that now grow only in warm countries, such as the persimmon. The great sequoia forest still covered the land, for it was during this period that there grew and were destroyed those fourteen fossil forests of the Yellowstone National Park (Figure 6-4).

Europe was much like America in those days. It consisted of low, flat hills and many shallow inland seas. At the beginning of the Miocene there were no snow-capped Alps. The general appearance of the flora of mid-Europe was probably much as it was on the shores of Lake Florissant in Colorado.

For a long time the Mediterranean Sea had been much larger than it is now. For millions of years in the Oligocene certain little creatures flourished in this warm and shallow body of water. They are called nummulites because they are so round and flat that they resemble the Roman coin *nummulus*. In some places these shells had accumulated until the deposits were one thousand feet thick and after millions of years were pressed into rock called limestone. During the Oligocene Period the land began to rise, for great changes were taking place all over the world. In the country we now call Egypt this limestone rock became dry land. Later by

Figure 17-1. Fossil leaves of the Miocene. The leaves of the plants are getting to be quite similar to our modern shrubs and trees.

(Smithsonian Institution)

perhaps a dozen million years the Egyptians cut this rock into blocks and made their pyramids.

During the latter part of the Miocene Period the apparently peaceful relations that had existed so long between the surface of the earth and the interior seemed to have come to a close, for all over the world there were long stretches of land, weak places in the earth's crust, where wrinkles occurred. Worse even that that — the layers of rock actually folded and cracked. So recent was this upheaval that these scars remain to this day. There are huge snow-capped mountains and cracks in the earth where the surfaces are still slipping past each other and causing earthquakes. In some cases, as along the east coast of North America where the Appalachian Mountains are now, the land merely rose and did not wrinkle or fold.

The Mississippi River flowed into the Gulf of Mexico at a point not far from that at which the city of Vicksburg now stands. All the southern coast was under water as far north as Virginia. Florida was submerged. The West Indies had again emerged from the sea and except for the presence of a few volcanoes began to look much as they do today. North and South America were once more connected by a land bridge that was considerably wider than the present Isthmus of Panama, but active volcanoes made its use as a bridge precarious.

On the West Coast the Gulf of California was larger than now and extended into territories we call California and Arizona. A remnant still existed of that strange land to the west of California. Oregon and Washington remained the scene of volcanic eruptions, which covered hundreds of thousands of square miles with lava and ashes. We have already found that this disturbance extended to the land of the Yellowstone National Park and to Lake Florissant in Colorado.

The coast of British Columbia and southern Alaska was very much as it is today, except that Bering Strait did not exist, for Asia and North America were connected by dry land. In the northeast, Greenland continued to be united to Canada, and the coast from New Jersey to Labrador extended farther eastward than now. The Gulf of St. Lawrence was smaller than now, and Hudson Bay did not exist.

There seems to be a constant struggle between the earth's crust and the air. The rock is ever wrinkling and folding and trying to erect lofty snow-capped mountains. The air, by its weapons of atoms and water and glaciers, is ever destroying these creations of the earth. The Greeks imagined such conflicts carried on by gods and goddesses called Titans. Javelins, lightning, and intrigue were used by them in geological conflicts. We have no Homer in modern geology to describe this conflict, greater than the siege of Troy. Perhaps Milton is our Homer, for he said:

"... And Chaos, ancestors of Nature, hold
Eternal anarchy, amidst the noise
Of endless wars, and by confusion stand.
For Hot, Cold, Moist, and Dry, four champions fierce,
Strive here for mastery, and to battle bring
Their embryon atoms.
... Chaos umpire sits,
And by decision more imbroils the fray
By which he reigns: next him, high arbiter,
Chance governs all."

Far back in Devonian times there were mountains in the country we now call California and Oregon. They soon lost in the conflict and were worn down to a peneplain. At the end of the Permian the earth again thrust up its crags on the west coast of British Columbia, Oregon, Washington, and California. However, the action of oxygen and the erosion by water and ice drove them back to well-rounded and wooded hills. Undaunted, in the Jurassic the earth wrinkled and created mountains in British Columbia and Idaho and made her first effort to raise the Sierra Nevada Mountains. But all in vain, for these peaks crumbled in millions of years as their predecessors had done. At the end of the Cretaceous Period the earth mustered her forces for a world-wide struggle and raised row on row of mountains where the Coast Range and Rocky Mountains are now. That air, "hot, cold, moist, and dry," always won, and during the long peaceful periods of the Eocene and Oligocene only low hills amid the forests and grassy plains were left to mark the earth's greatest efforts.

Now in the Miocene another conflict started, and the end of this struggle is not yet in sight. The earth wrinkled,

Figure 17-2.   A crack in the earth's surface near Darton, New Hampshire. Years ago the earth not only cracked but slipped, as shown by the displacement of the layers.   (U.S. Geological Survey)

cracked, and produced the Coast Range, the Sierra Nevada range, and the Rocky Mountains, with deep gulleys, valleys, and cliffs. As if to hurl defiance at the air, the earth threw out huge streams of lava from cracks formed by these upheavals. Upheavals they really were, for in California a great block of land hundreds of miles long tipped so that its eastern edge rose several thousand feet and its western edge sank into the land. It made the valley of California more prominent than before. This partly upturned block is called the Sierra Nevada Mountains. The two great cracks where the giant block rose on its eastern edge and sank on its western edge are still there. That block, the size of a state, is still uneasy. On the eastern edge every now and then it rises a little and the Sierra Nevada Mountains are pushed higher in the air. On March 26, 1872, this block rose twenty feet where the eastern crack occurs. The shock "was felt from Shasta to San Diego and points far beyond the border of Mexico. The tall trees of the Yosemite [valley] were waved about and bent like twigs, as the [earthquake] waves raced westward. Because of the sparse population, the casualties numbered fewer than 100, but the shock was probably much severer than the one that ruined so much of San Francisco in 1906. The air was charged with dust for a whole day. Owens Lake was jostled into turbulence and long, high foaming waves. Water fountains reaching seventy-five feet in height were spurted from the writhing fissures and many massive landslides occurred." So writes R. A. Daly in *Our Mobile Earth*.

All these upheavals were spread over vast periods of time. If any man had lived during the titanic disturbances, he would have said that the mountains were as eternal as the plains, for the slight movements accompanied sometimes by earthquakes would have seemed to him trivial. Yet through the long ages, by these trivial changes, the mountains rose and fell. Perhaps the Sierra Nevadas are rising today about as fast as they ever did; yet we think of them as "everlasting hills." Perhaps as one earthquake shock after another adds a few feet to their height, some day they may be the loftiest mountains in the world. Then in the course of millions of years the air will win the conflict, and there will be low hills and grassy plains instead of the beautiful Sierra Nevadas with snow-capped peaks and great valleys like the Yosemite National Park.

All over the world in the Miocene the earth began to writhe, squirm, wrinkle, and fold. The Andes rose again, for since their last effort at the end of the Cretaceous Period, they had been sadly destroyed by the perpetual nibbling of erosion. East and west wrinkles rose high in the air and then folded toward the north. Let us always remember, however, that the folding was ever so slow — probably no faster than the present rise of the Sierra Nevada Mountains; but after millions of years the effect was stupendous. Gullied by rain into innumerable valleys and torn by glaciers, the crumbling rock of these folds fell from their lofty heights. Now crags and broken peaks and terribly scarred mountains are all that is left of the magnificent folds that once rose against the air in serried ranks. One of the famous remnants is the Matterhorn in Switzerland. It is a portion of the front rank of a fold carried far north before the strength of the charge was exhausted.

While the uneasy earth was squirming and wrinkling under its blanket of air, no peace had settled down on the animal kingdom. The cats and dogs were becoming stronger, and the horses were growing larger and faster. It was a grim existence, in which most animals met with a violent death. During the Miocene, animals such as you see in Figure 17-3 roamed the plains. Although larger and swifter than his ancestors, Hypohippus, the Miocene horse (Figure 17-4), all too often served as food for the saber-toothed tiger.

Now in the Miocene a historic rival of the cat family asserts himself. Descended from a savage family of meat eaters known as the Miacidae, a kind of wild dog, Daphoenus (Fig-

Figure 17-3.   Animals of the Miocene Plains in what is now Nebraska. In the foreground, the huge-headed Dinohyus; at the right, feeding from the branches, Moropus; in the background, you will find a group of early horses, Parahippus, and a rhinoceros-like animal, Menoceras.

(© *Chicago Natural History Museum*)

ure 17-5), a powerful meat eater (sometimes called a "bear dog"), ranged the land. However, he was not destined to be the ancestor of man's best friend.

While cats and bear-dogs were Hypohippus's major troubles, he also had some minor tormentors; horseflies and other flies existed then as now. As if in contrast to the life of the

rest of the fauna, the butterflies, apparently at peace with the world, hovered over the flowers on the shores of Lake Florissant much as they do now in Colorado. However, the insect world had its terrors then as now, for S. H. Scudder found in

Figure 17-4. Hypohippus, a horse that lived in the forests of North America during the last part of the Miocene Period. After a drawing by C. R. Knight.   *(American Museum of Natural History)*

Figure 17-5. Daphoenus vetus, descended from Eocene creodonts called Miacidae, this small fox-like dog lived in North America during the early part of the Miocene Period. He is sometimes called a "bear-dog."

(© Chicago Natural History Museum)

the fossils of Lake Florissant the dreaded tsetse fly (Figure 17-6) that now kills so many thousands of people in Africa by means of a germ that it carries. This germ causes sleeping sickness, a dread disease, particularly fatal to cattle and to many other large animals. So the horse had another deadly enemy, and it is possible, according to H. F. Osborn, that the tsetse fly may have caused the complete disappearance of many large mammals that used to roam over the plains of North America. Perhaps these migrations of animals from Asia and Europe over those northern land bridges brought this deadly pest to America. Fortunately, this fly is now found only in certain parts of Africa and southern Arabia. In America he perished as completely as did his victims, the camels, horses, and rhinoceroses that used to inhabit this land by the tens of thousands. We are not at all sure that the mammals perished because of the fly, and as to tsetse himself, we have no idea why he became extinct in America, but we are very glad that he did.

How did our ancestors like this Miocene world? Did they grow stronger and more intelligent during these millions of years? Were there any more family differences of opinion that caused groups of conservatives to go off by themselves and live ever afterward as their ancestors had done? Apparently the answer to these questions is that the primates flourished during the Miocene, grew larger, stronger, brighter, and learned more about walking on the ground. Perhaps during this period they learned to defend themselves on the ground without always climbing that ancestral citadel, a tall tree. They traveled far and wide, for we find some of their jawbones and teeth in Spain, France, and India.

The change in climate had altered the dense forests of the Oligocene. Great plains of grass separated the tracts of woodlands. The primates that stayed in these temperate climates

Figure 17-6.   A remarkably well-preserved insect of the Miocene Period. It was caught in the mud of Lake Florissant, Colorado.

(American Museum of Natural History)

were forced to change their ways of living. The greater variety in their lives produced more brains, for those that were not bright enough to adapt themselves to new conditions perished.

Those primates who could just reach the Miocene stage but could go no further we call great apes; they are living now in Africa, and there apparently they still find conditions much as they were back in the Miocene. They have now separated into several groups, but they all have a strong family resemblance, and perhaps they resemble our common ancestors. We have given the name Dryopithecus to this group of ape ancestors who lived in the Miocene of Asia, Europe, and Africa and the Pliocene of Europe and Asia.

The gorillas (Figure 17-7) and the chimpanzees now living in Africa probably together give us a very good idea of the degree of intelligence of their great-grandfather Dryopithecus. The expression of his face and the way he walked is possibly fairly well represented by the combination of gorilla and chimpanzee.

Do not think that life in the Miocene consisted only of the animals we have mentioned; there were many, many more, such as rhinoceroses, venomous snakes, deer, and bison. Our space is limited, however, so that we must write no more about this interesting 20 million years of the "Less Recent."

Figure 17-7.   A male gorilla in all his splendor. Carl Akeley, a student of these magnificent animals, reported that gorillas are not savage — unless attacked.   (*American Museum of Natural History*)

18

The Pliocene Period

The Pliocene Period — meaning "More Recent" — began ten million years ago and lasted nine million years. It was a time of rising of lands, increasing cold, and the migration of huge mammals called mastodons.

After our long journey and intimate contact with the magnificent creations of the animal kingdom, we feel sad as we reach that time when the modern era first begins to take shape. As we look about us, we see our fellow men exterminating the animal kingdom at an incredible and needless rate. Not many generations from now and certainly in our present geological period, only those large animals will be left that are kept in reservations or carefully bred for man's use. Evolution in the animal kingdom will have ceased except as man will have directed its course by the careful selection of those whose special characteristics he wishes to retain.

During the nine million years of the "More Recent," the land of North America rose to a considerable extent, so that the continent began to look very much like the maps in geography books. Greenland, toward the end of the period, became entirely separated from Canada. The depression that allowed the water to flow between these great bodies of land

and to connect the Arctic Ocean with the Atlantic did not extend to the east coast of North America; for then, as for several periods in the past, the coast line extended far out to sea, in some cases for one hundred miles. Those historic rivers, the St. Lawrence, Hudson, Delaware, and James, still joined the Atlantic Ocean far to the east where now fishes swim in several hundred feet of water.

Florida had ceased to be an island and looked very much like a peninsula, but it did not extend so far south as at present. The West Indies, on the other hand, were almost modern in appearance, at least so far as their outline was concerned. North and South America were still united, but the land bridge was not so wide as in the Miocene. Those volcanoes that must have terrified the migrating animals were still there. In fact, a zone of active volcanoes extended all up the Pacific Coast as far as the southern part of British Columbia. Then they appeared again in Alaska, where they are found to this day.

The Mississippi River still flowed into the Gulf of Mexico at a point not far from the modern city of Vicksburg. It had to begin to cut a channel again, for the whole valley rose several hundred feet during this period.

The Pacific Coast began to look much as it does now except that the coast line was in most cases farther to the west than at present. The Rocky Mountains continued to rise and at the end of this period reached nearly their present height. That partly upturned block that began to raise its eastern edge high in the air in the Miocene continued to tip and to rise even more in this period. The rainwater, as it drained off over the western slope of this unsettled block, cut deep gullies that became large V-shaped valleys with steep sides. In the next period the cold became so intense that glaciers were formed, and these V-shaped valleys were gouged and scraped into U-shaped valleys. This upturned block of land, as big as a state, and these deep rain-washed valleys turning to U-shaped valleys made some of the grandest scenery in the world. Yosemite National Park contains one of these valleys (Figure 10-7).

You have probably heard of the Great American Desert, which lies east of the Sierra Nevada Mountains and between them and the Rocky Mountains. This stretch of desolation was caused by that upturned block of land, the Sierra Nevada Mountains. The wind in that part of the country usually blows from the west. On its way over the Pacific Ocean it has picked up many of those little globules of water that we have described in connection with glaciers. When this wind tries to climb over the tops of the Sierra Nevada Mountains, it loses them, for when air rises to the top of a mountain, it becomes cold. Then it cannot hold so many globules of water, and they fall as snowflakes or raindrops. Consequently, when the air has passed over the mountains and started on its journey east, it is nearly dry and can give scarcely any rain. Such a condition always causes a desert, and a desert we have to the east of the Sierra Nevada Mountains even to this day. Also that desert will be there until the mountains are again worn down to a peneplain and once more the moist air from off the Pacific can blow over the low wooded hills and bring rain to the thirsty country. As they have done in some other deserts, men some day may bring water in canals and pipes from distant mountains and thus defy the Sierra Nevadas.

This new rise of the Rocky Mountains and the Sierra Nevadas also raised the land between them by several thousand feet. The Colorado River began at once to cut a new and deeper channel as it flowed over its ancient course on this plateau. It has been undermining its banks and carrying the debris downstream for several million years, and now has cut a canyon a mile deep — the most wonderful canyon in the world (Figure 18-1).

Far back in the Eocene there developed a family of little elephants that must have had ancestors among the archaic mammals of the Cretaceous Period and perhaps even earlier. The oldest member of this family that has ever been found lived in Egypt on the banks of the primitive Nile, sometimes called the Ur-Nile. This elephant's name is Moeritherium (Figure 18-2). He was about the size of a tapir and was fond of bathing.

Figure 18-1.   The Grand Canyon — a mile deep. Do you see the Colorado River that has been cutting this deep channel canyon for several million years?   (Union Pacific Railroad Photo)

Figure 18-2.   Moeritherium, a primitive elephant, was about the size of a tapir. He lived part of the time in the water and is the most ancient elephant so far discovered. He may have lived as far back as the Eocene. After a drawing by C. R. Knight under the direction of H. F. Osborn at the American Museum of Natural History.

(American Museum of Natural History)

The members of that elephant family were as marvelous in some respects as their successors, the Egyptian primates who carved the Sphinx. Unlike the Egyptians, the elephants were pioneers and explorers. They traveled far and wide wherever they could walk. Of the sixteen different groups of elephants that originated in Egypt or perhaps in some cases in India, eleven reached America. "An insatiable wanderlust," says H. F. Osborn, "has always possessed the souls of elephants as it has those of the tribes and races of man. Not only to overcome the changes and chances of this mortal life, but also to gratify their intelligent curiosity ever to explore fresh forests, pastures, fields, rivers and streams they have gone to the very ends of the earth and have far surpassed man in adapting their clothing and teeth to all possible conditions of life. Thus the romances of elephant migration and conquest are second only to the romances of human migration and conquest."

Several of the groups of elephants were so much alike that we call them all mastodons. The earliest mastodon that has left us his skeleton was Phiomia (Figure 18-3). He lived in

Egypt in the Oligocene Period, and his descendants, as they carried out the traditions of this Viking family, grew larger and traveled farther. Their jaws, always long, became longer. Finally before the end of the Miocene these elephants reached South Dakota. They had traveled by way of Siberia and Alaska and had spent several million years on the journey. Then there were mastodons famous for their peculiar teeth ("serrate-toothed," Figure 18-4). Apparently, like European white primates, a large number tried to come to Canada and America, and many of them succeeded.

The old contest between the horse and the cat continued during this period. The horses grew large, swift, and numerous. Hipparion is the name of the leading horse of the Pliocene. At last he had a hoof as any self-respecting horse should have. It took him 50 million years to lose those four useless

Figure 18-3. Way back in the Oligocene of Egypt the descendants of Phiomia inherited her long jaws. As time went on and the family traveled far, they grew larger and the family characteristic grew more pronounced. Restorations by Osborn and Knight at the American Museum of Natural History. H. F. Osborn was the discoverer of Phiomia.

(American Museum of Natural History)

Figure 18-4.   A serrate-toothed mastodon is pictured above. This fellow died in what is now Texas in the Pliocene. He was about six feet high and was fond of leaves. His family left home in the Miocene Period and traveled by way of Gobi, where one of his relatives died and left a jawbone for the expedition of the American Museum of Natural History. After a painting by C. R. Knight.   (*American Museum of Natural History*)

toes and develop a hoof. Therefore, we must not be surprised if we find that we humans have changed little since the time of the Greeks or even the Egyptians; what are a few thousand years compared with the 50 million years required by the horse to lose four toes?

During this period the saber-tooth cat apparently increased in size. Late in the next period these wonderful creatures died; they left no descendants. They had been 60 million years developing from the savage meat-eating creodonts. Then they suddenly vanished, for reasons unknown. About the same time the vast herds of horses and the innumerable camels and rhinoceroses became nearly extinct as far as North America was concerned. Apparently some camels, at least, survived through the Pleistocene Period, according to a discovery recently made in Utah and described by A. S. Romer of the University of Chicago in *Science* of June 6, 1928. Other animals came to take their places, such as the bear, royal bison, and the *Mastodon americanus*. Smilodon (Figure 19-3) and Machairodus had spent so many million years in reaching tiger perfection that we cannot help a feeling of regret at their untimely death. If they had lived one period longer, our immediate ancestors would have had the pleasure of meeting them.

Over in Asia there were developed at this time some mammals that were destined to prove as useful as the horse. They were the cattle. Those that man has domesticated never migrated over the land bridge of Siberia and Alaska as did the mastodons and some of the early mammals. They were brought to North America in boats from Europe only when the European white primates made the last great mammal migration to America.

We have reserved till the last in this chapter the most important animals of all, the primates. With the increasingly cold weather, the forests slowly lost their tropical appearance. Those primates that did not migrate to warmer lands had to be constantly changing their mode of living. Of course, as usual, the change was made by the relentless law of the elimination of the unfit. During the next period they evidently learned not only to defend themselves on the ground but also to use tools of some crude kind; and late in the period, it is thought by some, they used sharp-pointed and sharp-edged stones as scrapers for the preparation of the furs that they may have used for added warmth, for during the final part of this period they may have protected themselves from cold by the use of skins of other animals. Such progressive primates we call men and women, or human beings.

This is another subject on which there is a wide difference of opinion. When did our ancestors begin to use sharp-pointed stones and stone scrapers? J. Reid Moir in England has discovered a great many pieces of flint of this period that he thinks were made by those progressive primates or early men, and a number of distinguished geologists agree with him. Some of these flints are kept in the British Museum. Yet it is not certain that they were chipped by man. They may have been broken by ordinary wear and tear of the weather and by the pressure of rocks. From time to time you will probably learn about new investigations, and some day you may know just when your ancestors were bright enough to chip stones into sharp points for use as tools.

Figure 18-5.   Three who preceded you. Left, Pithecanthropus, still an ape-man. Center, Neanderthal man, definitely a man. Right, Cro-Magnon man, easily recognizable — and quite handsome.

(American Museum of Natural History)

19

The Pleistocene Period

We come now to the last period in the earth's history. It is called Pleistocene, meaning "Most Recent," and is the shortest of all the periods; it started about one million years ago. So far as we are concerned, it is the most eventful epoch in the history of the earth. During this brief and stormy time the primates whom we call men and women developed very rapidly. From being barely able to stand erect, use a wooden club, and perhaps make crude flint tools, they became men who dressed themselves in skins and were able to paint on the walls of caves colored pictures that are the admiration of artists even today.

In 1903 Dr. Dubois of Holland discovered in Java most of the skull, some of the teeth, and one bone of a Pleistocene primate. By comparing these bones with those of other primates and with the skeletons of other very early men, it has been possible to draw a fair picture of this contemporary of our ancestors. His name is Pithecanthropus (Figure 18-5), and his portrait should be hung in our dining-room.

W. D. Matthew, former professor of palaeontology, University of California, has published in *Natural History* (Vol. XXVIII) a very interesting story of a group of such ape-men as Pithecanthropus: "Three ape-men come trotting down one of the trails, tall, upright, broad-shouldered, their gleaming brown skin half concealed by sparse black hair. They run at an easy jog-trot, steady, watchful, with quick, flashing glances to right and left, noting the least sound or movement in the forest, a broken leaf by the trail, a displaced branch underfoot.

"Every now and then they slow down to a walk or stop to examine some new or unusual object, track, or mark, crowding around it to see better, pointing and gesturing and expressing ideas in a sort of rude language of clicks and grunts . . . .

"A movement and rustle in a leafy covert brings a shower of heavy and well-directed stones, which serves to dislodge a tiger lurking there. He springs for the moment into the open, then slinks off, bruised and battered, well aware that he stands but little chance of coming to close quarters with these active, wily enemies, who at last resort could always scramble up a tree out of reach and thence continue the attack with sticks and branches. The tiger driven off, the ape-men amuse themselves by pestering some of the smaller animals, routing out some of them from their holes or sheltered corners around the roots of a tree, and exchanging missiles and abuse with a troop of monkeys in the tree-tops. . . .

"Does this rude sketch sound like the escapades of a gang of bad little boys? I hope so. Because that is just what the ape-men were, as I think of them. Clever and restless, mischievous, inconsequent, irresponsible, somehow I can't help liking them in spite of their naughtiness. And with the spirit of the gamin was combined the strength and hardiness and independence of the grown man, the savage and bestial face of the great apes, but the body and limbs of quite human type, only clothed with more or less of a coat of hair. A singular combination, based, as we shall see, upon very scanty evidence, yet I think on the whole the most probable concept that we can build up from such facts as are to be had. Some day, when Java or other regions of central and southern Asia have been more extensively explored for fossils, we shall know how near this picture is to fact."

With the close of this period comes the end of the successive supremacies of the great fishes, reptiles, and four-footed mammals. In the next chapter we shall find the irresistible power of the progressive primates already asserting itself. These primates in the next period will develop to such an extent that they will understand a large part of the law of evolution. Then they will use it as a tool for their own advantage. As ruthlessly as *Tyrannosaurus rex* or Smilodon, they will eliminate all animals, fish, flesh, or fowl, that oppose their progress. From their knowledge of evolution they will carefully select the parents, that the offspring may suit man's convenience. Thus they will raise hens that will lay an incredible number of eggs, and horses with a speed greater than that imparted by a fear of Smilodon.

The Pleistocene is also known as the Ice Age. Great glaciers came and went during this million years. In America, the last glacier disappeared from the region of New York City about 38,000 years ago and in Europe from the southern part of Sweden about 12,000 years ago. Parts of the great glaciers are still found in Greenland, the northeastern part of North America, and the Antarctic Continent. Until we can roam through a forest-covered Greenland on our summer vacations, we cannot claim that the Ice Age is entirely past, for you remember that during nearly all the 1,000 million years of the earth's history, Greenland has been a warm country with thick forests. To have Greenland covered with a huge glacier is unusual from a geological point of view, and, geologically speaking, is probably a temporary condition.

Those mysterious glaciers began to form in Canada and Greenland at the beginning of the Pleistocene Period. After thousands of years the ice spread far and wide and began to cover the northern states. The wind took tens of thousands of years to evaporate from the ocean enough little globules of the water, which, when turned into snowflakes and then into ice, made this giant glacier. And giant it really was, for in some places in Canada it may have been 10,000 feet thick — two miles of solid ice.

Then Canada became warmer; the globules of water fell as rain instead of snow. Slowly, very slowly, the ice melted and disappeared. Four and perhaps five times the ice came and went, and each invasion and withdrawal took an interminable time; altogether more than a million years of the earth's history are involved in these mighty pulsations.

These glaciers were destructive phenomena, more destructive than any of the fauna, even than *Tyrannosaurus rex* or Charalarodon. They withered the forests by their blighting cold and then tore up the ground and piled it high in the form of hills of gravel. They changed the courses of rivers, and when they melted and withdrew, left lakes where before there had been dry land.

When the glacier reached its farthest south in North America, a large part of the country now called Canada and the United States was under ice. Each time the glacier came south, it stayed as an unwelcome visitor for tens of thousands of years and held as prisoners all those vast clouds of water globules that made its ice.

If the primates could have published geographies in Europe

at this time, they would have drawn some very queer maps. The receding water had exposed the ocean bottom for hundreds of miles from the present coast line. Certainly you would not have recognized Europe at all. A broad belt of land extended from the countries we call France and Germany northwest to Greenland. That famous river, the Rhine, flowed north into the Arctic Ocean, and the Thames was probably a branch of the Rhine. The Seine River flowed into a deep gorge we speak of as the English Channel River. This river flowed through a valley or canyon whose sides rose hundreds of feet. These rivers tumbled into the Atlantic Ocean through gorges that were much like the Colorado canyon of today, only on a smaller scale. There must have been wild scenery in those glacial days.

At the Straits of Gibraltar the water was shallow. When the ocean's level was lowered because of the stealing of water by the glaciers, this land was exposed and became a land bridge that connected Europe and Africa. Then a curious thing happened to the Mediterranean Sea, for it began to dry up. In the Mediterranean today, the water evaporates faster than it can be supplied by such rivers as the Danube, Nile, and Rhone. If it were not for the connection with the Atlantic Ocean at Gibraltar, it would evaporate so rapidly that it would become a series of large lakes instead of an inland sea. This is just what happened in the glacial epoch. There was a land bridge connecting Italy, Sicily, and Africa and another that connected Greece with Asia Minor.

Of course all this new land was not due to the stealing of the water from the ocean by the glaciers. A great deal of this change in the map was caused by the rise of the land.

Like an irresistible horde of conquering globules that had massed together in giant blocks of ice, the European glaciers devastated the land almost as extensively and quite as slowly as did the American glaciers. Growing larger and larger in Norway and Sweden, they extended as far as London and covered all Denmark and part of northern Germany. At the same time another great ice sheet spread from the Alps and covered all of the country we now call Switzerland and parts of Germany, France, Austria, and Italy. Nearly all the island of Corsica was under a glacier. As in North America, these European glaciers appeared and disappeared four times during the Pleistocene Period.

Thick furs were very fashionable garments for the fauna in the Pleistocene days. Herds of reindeer and huge woolly mam-

Figure 19-1. Picture of an American mastodon. Fossil remains of this animal are found throughout the eastern and central states. Many specimens have been discovered in draining swamplands about Chicago. From a restoration by C. R. Knight.   *(American Museum of Natural History)*

moths crossed the frozen rivers of France when the ice sheets were descending from the Alps. In North America, the *Mastodon americanus* (Figure 19-1) wandered over the land in herds of several hundreds as the modern buffalo used to do on our western plains

Another animal not dressed for warm weather is the musk ox (Figure 19-2). Now he is found only on the shores of the Arctic Ocean. In the Pleistocene, however, he ate moss and grass in New Jersey and Kentucky.

Our old friend the saber-tooth tiger disappeared during this period. Smilodon and Machairodus were the last leaders of this powerful branch of the cat family (Figure 19-3). The

Figure 19-2.   A very thick fur protects a musk ox from the cold of the Arctic Circle where he now lives, although in the Pleistocene Period he roamed over Virginia and Kentucky.

(Frank Dufresne, U.S. Fish and Wildlife Service)

Figure 19-3.   The saber-tooth cat, Smilodon, lived in North and South America during the first part of the Pleistocene Period. Fortunately for us, he no longer roams through the forests. From a painting by C. R. Knight.
(American Museum of Natural History)

Figure 19-4.   Equus Scotti is his name. He was the last of his race, until the Spaniards brought his cousins from Europe to Texas. After a painting by C. R. Knight.   *(American Museum of Natural History)*

peace-loving American horse (Figure 19-4) disappeared with the tiger, and many of them doubtless disappeared into the tiger.

Near the present city of Los Angeles there was in this period a "tar-pool" still in existence, which acted as a cruel trap for all these animals. If an animal ventured too far on its surface in search of food, he invariably got caught and slowly sank into the tar. It was as dangerous as the quicksands in some of our ponds and on an occasional beach. The more the victims struggled, the deeper they sank. Their cries must have echoed through the forest, for other animals came not to help but to devour them. Then these last comers in their turn became entangled in the pool. Thousands of bones have been dug from this spot and are now in the museum in Los Angeles.

Perhaps it was during the long warm times between those four great ice periods that the Imperial Mammoth lived in Nebraska and Texas (Figure 19-5), for he apparently did not have such a warm fur coat as *Mastodon americanus*. He was a majestic creature and looks as if he were proud of the great plains over which his rule was supreme.

When the ice melted, retreated to the north, and finally disappeared from nearly all of the continent of North America, great changes would have been necessary in maps if any had been printed in those days. A sheet of ice covering several million square miles, and from one to two miles thick, such as the one shown in Figure 19-6, has enormous weight. It would crush almost anything, and the earth's crust actually did bend under the load. The coasts of Labrador, Nova Scotia, and Maine were pushed far under the water, although the level of the ocean was lower, as we have seen, than it used to be. New beaches were cut by the waves. Then after the ice had gone and the land rose again, these beaches were raised and now you find them hundreds of feet above the sea, which again is busy cutting new beaches at its present level.

Because the land was pushed down by the weight of the ice, the water from the melting glacier sometimes formed pools where the land was depressed. As the ice melted, these pools overflowed and became the source of some of our largest rivers. The more the ice melted and the ice sheet retreated north, the larger some of these pools grew. Finally, they became our Great Lakes. The map in Figure 19-6 not only shows the huge ice sheet but also shows places where an earlier glacier had retreated; there it had already begun the business of gouging out the basins which were to form our Great Lakes.

Figure 19-5.   Imperial Mammoth of Nebraska and Texas after a painting by C. R. Knight in the American Museum of Natural History.

(American Museum of Natural History)

Figure 19-6.   The upper right represents the great ice sheet that covered part of Canada and parts of the United States. As it retreated, it gouged out the Great Lakes.   (*U.S. Geological Survey*)

After the ice melted, the land rose very slowly to nearly its former height, but it has never returned entirely to its first position; perhaps some day it will. At one time, just as the ice had melted and the land was still considerably depressed where the ice had been, the Atlantic Ocean flowed in to take the place of the melting glacier. The ocean flowed up the Gulf of St. Lawrence as far as that great ice pool that we call Lake Ontario. It flowed south over the country now occupied by Lake Champlain and the Hudson River Valley, so that New England was an island. Whales must have circumnavigated this island, for one of them became stranded and left his skeleton on a beach of Lake Champlain.

Like a rubber ball that has been dented, the crust of the earth gradually recovered from the terrific weight of the glacier. Then as the land rose, the old beaches rose with it, and New England was no longer an island. We are not surprised then to learn that the whale's skeleton was found on one of these raised beaches several hundred feet above the present surface of Lake Champlain.

As our story comes to a close, let us study our own family history and learn, if we can, when and where our immediate ancestors, the European primates, first appear. We have followed the development of the primates from a small tree-living animal, which lived 50 to 100 million years ago, to the ape type of animal that walked on his hind legs and perhaps in the late Pleistocene Period chipped pieces of flint he probably used as tools to assist him in preparing skins for his protection against the cold.

When a primate becomes sufficiently intelligent to use sticks and crudely worked stones as tools or weapons, we call him a man. Man-primates and ape-primates had a common ancestry.

Life during the million years of the Pleistocene became very strenuous for the primates in the Northern Hemisphere. The encroachment of the grassy plains on the forests caused many migrations among our forest-loving ancestors. Also those great pulsations of advancing and retreating ice sheets forced the primates either to move to other climates or rather radically to change their mode of living. Probably both these things happened. The great territories, Europe, Africa, and North America, that were connected with Central Asia by land bridges, were time after time invaded by primates.

The first European of the Pleistocene who was kind enough to leave his bones for our museums lived in Germany near the place now made famous by the great University of Heidelberg, and he is known as the Heidelberg Man. In those days Europe was warm, for the first glacier had come and gone.

Europe probably enjoyed a climate milder than at present. The Heidelberg Man or his ancestors had wandered far in the search for food. Perhaps they had followed the retreating ice until after tens of thousands of years they arrived in the country that we now call Germany.

Perhaps the men of the Ice Age came to Europe in several waves of migration during thousands of years, for we find that their ways of living changed rather suddenly from time to time, as if there had been new arrivals from Asia with new ideas. Historical America has been settled in about the same way, but during a much shorter period. You know that in some of our cities the first European settlers were English. The next wave of migration a hundred years later was Irish, and finally a third migration of Italians came, perhaps fifty years later. The English, Irish, and Italians, though all Europeans, have slightly different ways of living. So it may be that many of the successive waves of early man that overran Europe during the Pleistocene Period were all related to a primitive Asiatic group. But this is an educated guess; we need more facts.

Just as we speak of waves of English, Irish, or Italian immigrants, so these successive settlers in Europe have received separate names. Among the first and most primitive are the Chelleans, named after the place where their stone tools were first found. They lived in Europe during the warm period that followed the third series of glaciers that spread over the land. The flint tools or scrapers that the Chelleans have left behind them show that they used the fur of such animals as the reindeer and bear to keep themselves warm. All the flints they have left in their camps and caves were apparently used for domestic purposes. No arrowheads or spear points have been found. They probably used a pointed stick for a spear, but they knew nothing about the bow and arrow.

The invention of even crude clothing was one of the most important achievements of the primates. Apparently the primates who gradually became men had lived for so many million years in a warm climate that they had almost completely lost their own fur — we still have a little on the tops of our heads. If, then, they were to follow their favorite game into countries where there was snow and ice in winter, they must devise some form of clothing.

About this time primitive man made another invention of far-reaching importance. It was the use of fire. This invention also was probably made primarily for warmth. Later, of course, primitive men and women learned to prefer roasted meat to raw meat.

Both fire and clothing were probably used by primitive men and women long before the Chelleans appeared in Europe. Perhaps these inventions were made in Asia and brought to Europe, Africa, and America by successive waves of migrating primates. We only know that the first undisputed evidences of well-formed flint tools for dressing skins and, according to Hugo Obermaier, the first clear evidence of the use of fire are found in the old Chellean camps and caves of Europe.

Then came the fourth great glacier, which covered a large part of Europe with ice for perhaps 100,000 years. This series of glaciers, radiating from the Alps and from Scandinavia, moved so slowly that for thousands of years the climate grew colder very gradually. It was during this time that a new group of tribes came into Europe and apparently displaced the old Chellean inhabitants. We call them Acheuleans. They have left behind them better flint tools than the Chelleans could make. They must have been better fighters, too, for all traces of the old Chelleans disappeared with the appearance of the Acheuleans.

The next invasion of Europe that we know about was made by men certainly more intelligent and perhaps more numerous. It was just before the fourth and last advance of the glaciers that these men, wonderful for those days, entered Europe. It may be that they came from Asia Minor, crossed the Bosphorus where Constantinople now stands, and entered Europe by walking up the broad valley of the Danube. Remains of these men have been found in a cave in Palestine by John Garstang of the University of Liverpool and in the Danube Valley by other explorers. This immigration is called Mousterian, and the people of this race are called Neanderthals (Figure 18-5). There is some reason to believe, according to W. J. Sollas of Oxford University, that when these Neanderthals went northwest to Europe, others of the same or similar race went southeast, where they perhaps lived until other men came and caused their extinction. You must remember that the evidence of this migration and those described below is not always clear. There is a great deal of educated guesswork, but it is based on conflicting evidence.

Many places in Europe where they lived during the Mousterian epoch have been investigated, and the charred remains of their feasts have been found. We know what animals they liked to eat, but do not think for a moment that the meat they ate was always fresh. Meat so old that we could not have it within smelling distance was probably enjoyed by them at their feasts. When these men of Europe had finished eating a carcass, they just threw what was left a short distance from their campfire. They had no garbage heap they burned or kept carefully covered with earth. The smell of badly decayed remains did not, apparently, disturb them. Around one of their camps the bones of a couple of thousand animals have been found, buried by the sand of ages, but lying as they had been thrown by these Neanderthal men of the Mousterian epoch.

The Neanderthal men and women came to Europe at an unfortunate time. The fourth and last great glacier was commencing to cover much of the land. Since these Neanderthals of the Mousterian immigration did not know how to build warm houses, they lived in caves, where they could keep large fires burning at the entrances. Mankind made little progress during the thousands of years of the fourth invasion of the Pleistocene ice. They did not make their stone tools so well at the end of the icy period as they did at the beginning. Whatever the reasons may have been, the Neanderthal of the Mousterian migration was not able to resist the next great wave of mankind that entered Europe.

Apparently Europe was invaded this time from two directions and by two somewhat different types of mankind. A tall race, standing more erect than the Neanderthals, perhaps came from the east and entered Europe through the historic gateway, the Danube Valley. The other race came from Africa, crossed the Mediterranean on those land bridges, and occupied southern Europe.

During the next epoch, called Aurignacian, these two races occupied Europe. The old Neanderthals disappeared. Most of them probably perished while fighting the new invaders, for the Aurignacian people used a wonderful invention, the bow and arrow.

These two races that dwelt in Europe during the Aurignacian epoch produced the first artists of whom we have any knowledge. Their drawings were made on the smooth rock walls in the caves. At first the pictures were crudely drawn, but the race grew more skillful as each thousand-year period was added to its history.

For thousands of years these two races, witnessing, it may

be, the very dawn of art in the human race, occupied Europe. The more they decorated their caves and drew pictures on stag's horns and on ivory, the more skillful they became. So far as we know, only once was their possession of Europe seriously disputed. That disturbance was for a brief time when a tribe of good fighters came up the valley of the Danube as the Neanderthal man had done tens of thousands of years before. These new men are called Solutreans. They made poor pictures but very sharp spears. For a short while, apparently, they ruled Europe, and then they disappeared. Whether they were driven away or killed we do not know.

We do know that again artistic races occupied Europe. Those little men and women from northern Africa still lived in southern Europe, for they never had been driven out by the Solutreans. In the north and central parts we find the remains of a tall giant race very much like their predecessors. We call them Cro-Magnons (Figure 18-5). They may have been cousins but not descendants of the original big men of the Aurignacian epoch. There is some evidence that these tall and erect Cro-Magnons first appeared in Spain and then spread west and northwest through Europe. With the Cro-Magnons in this epoch was a shorter type that bears some resemblance to our modern Eskimo.

The second epoch in the life of these artistic races is called the Magdalenian. In no other period in any part of the earth did early man produce such works of art. These Magdalenian artists of the Cro-Magnon race used colors in making lifelike pictures of animals (Figure 19-7). They carved in ivory and modeled in clay.

Finally the Cro-Magnon men devised a way of representing a herd of reindeer without drawing each animal. Having started the picture of the herd with a few well-drawn deer, they found a series of lines sufficient to suggest to the mind

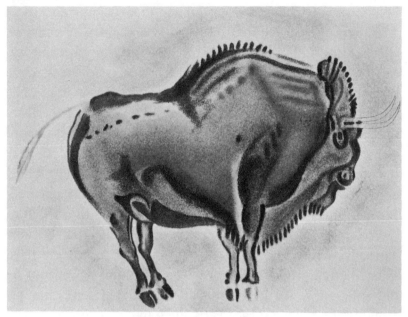

Figure 19-7.   This beautiful drawing of a bison was found in the caves of Altamira, Spain. Cro-Magnon man was probably the artist.

(American Museum of Natural History)

the idea of a stampeding herd of wild reindeer. They used the same impressionistic method to represent a herd of galloping horses.

While Cro-Magnon were developing this remarkable skill and were using bone needles and other tools (Figure 19-8) that have been found in their camps, the fourth and last great Pleistocene glacier was slowly withdrawing from Europe. For thousands of years this glacier or, to be more accurate, this group of glaciers slowly melted. In Switzerland some shrank away up the valleys between the remnants of those majestic folds that had risen in the Miocene Period. The slowly moving ice sheets that are so characteristic of Alpine scenery today are merely miniature images of their giant predecessors. In northern Germany and Great Britain the glaciers withdrew toward the north, and there beyond the Arctic Circle we find them today. This withdrawal of the last Pleistocene glaciers was not uniform. There were times when for a hundred years or more the glaciers grew neither larger nor smaller. We have a similar situation today, for we find the glaciers of Switzerland have changed very little in size during the period of modern history. Then there were times when the glaciers grew larger and extended farther down the valleys or, in Germany and Great Britain, covered more land. The glaciers, like huge frozen monsters, seemed reluctant to retreat from Europe and North America under the repeated attacks of the increasingly warm air. Just as the air had always won in its conflict with the mountains, so the warm air gradually melted the ice and drove the glacier to its final stand near the tops of the high mountains and in the distant polar regions.

Figure 19-8. These tools and ornaments were used by the men and women who were our ancestors.   *(American Museum of Natural History)*

With the withdrawal of the glaciers, great changes in the weather probably took place throughout the world. During the Cro-Magnon epoch and presumably for a long time before that period, the country we now call Egypt enjoyed a moist climate with many storms and plenty of rain. The great Nile River, destined to be so famous, had dried up because the sources of the river in far-off Abyssinia and Central Africa were nearly dry. Strange rivers ran across the old Nile Valley from the hills that lie to the east and along the edge of the Red Sea.

With the disappearance of the glaciers the weather changed. Abyssinia had once more a season of heavy rainfall. This rain water drained into the numerous rivers that make the sources of the Nile, which again flowed north through its historic valley to the Mediterranean Sea. The winds that brought rain to Egypt and caused those rivers to flow from the Red Sea hills across the Nile Valley disappeared. A dry northerly wind took their place, and Egypt became again the sandy waste with which we are now so familiar.

The return of the Nile to its former glory took place about 12,000 B.C. The glacier left the northern shores of Germany about 15,000 B.C. and in its retreat north finally abandoned the southern shores of Sweden about 10,000 B.C. For reasons that we cannot give in this story, these dates are known with fair accuracy. However, more important to us than these dates or the movements of the glacier are the great migrations of primitive men that were apparently caused by changing weather. Perhaps the interior of Asia grew dry so that the animals were forced to seek food to the west in Europe and to the east in North America. In that case the meat-eating primates would certainly follow the animals.

Whatever the cause, the artistic career of the Cro-Magnon people came to a close with the invasion into Europe of primitive men from Russia and Asia. They came up the valley of the Danube River, and they came along the shores of the Baltic Sea. They were better fighters than the Cro-Magnons and had sharper spears. These invading warriors were soon followed by men who had domestic dogs and knew how to make dishes out of clay.

Once before, the life of these cave artists had been interrupted by the Solutrean warriors. Finally, at the time of the appearance of the modern Nile and the disappearance of the old glacier, the Cro-Magnons were crushed by the invading hordes of fighters from Russia and Asia. Yet they were not exterminated as were their predecessors, the Neanderthal men. Although no longer making remarkable pictures and statues, they lived with their conquerors. Even today there is some reason to believe there are thousands of people in southern France who are descended from that wonderful race of artists.

Now we have almost reached the epoch when human beings kept records. Ten thousand years more or less bring us to the present time. During this interval man has made tremendous progress. Like the mammals and reptiles of old, he has migrated in large numbers from one continent to another. Since he can sail over the ocean, he no longer needs the ancient land bridges, some of which have sunk beneath the sea. The animals, however, have changed very little since Cro-Magnon man drew pictures of horses on the walls of his cave.

One of the principal reasons for this lack of change is the shortness of the time. We must always remember that it usually takes millions of years to bring about important changes in animals, as well as in mountains. Also in this very brief period of a few thousand years, there have been no marked changes in climate. No great mountain chains have risen or disappeared. No large land mass has sunk beneath the sea or risen from it. No new glacier has spread over the land. Therefore, there is no reason why most of the animals should change in so short a time.

We have covered 1,000 million years (perhaps 1,500 million years) of the earth's history. We did not start at the beginning, and now we must bring our story to a close before we have reached the present time.

20

An Imaginary Period

We have finished our story. We started when the earth was a magnificent ball, huge shooting stars were falling into a boiling ocean, the clouds were brilliant with lightning, and thunder echoed among the newly made mountains as the earth squirmed and writhed under the blows from those falling stars. It was a wonderful time, when only the laws of physics and chemistry were in control.

Then as Sam and the rest of us traveled down through the museums of time, we saw our early microscopic ancestors appear in the warm fresh water of those very early oceans. We saw living things develop from a single cell into a group of cells. In turn, there have appeared before us the fish, the amphibian, the reptile, and the mammal. Finally, from among the mammals there appeared the primates and from among the primates the European primates who founded the British Empire and the United States of America.

We have watched mountain ranges come and go. Several times we have shivered as we realized that the glaciers were creeping down over a large part of the earth. Through long ages we have seen great stretches of land slowly disappear beneath the ocean, and then we have welcomed other land masses as they rose from the sea.

Do you suppose we all realize how long these changes have taken — how very, very slowly the earth moves and the animals change? The whole history of America and even of Europe is but a day compared with the time that has passed since primates first came down from trees in search of food.

Perhaps you are still puzzled by that perplexing question we have encountered so frequently: Why do some animals develop new shapes and habits, while at the same time their cousins do not change at all? Apparently no animal ever changes his shape very much unless starvation or death continually selects certain ones that are different from their brothers and sisters; then, after ages, new animals are evolved.

As we have examined the earth in this imaginary journey, we have seen our ancestors change from using fins to using feet and walking on the dry ground. Then they stood on their hind legs and developed hands. During all this time they had some brains — very little, to be sure. As they grew more intelligent, the primates gained ascendancy, using their brains to advantage. Brain and muscle were used together. There are usually two ways by which animals accomplish their tasks. First, an animal can accomplish his purpose by brute force, or, secondly, he can accomplish the same thing by using his brains. *Tyrannosaurus rex* and Smilodon used brute force principally, but the primates use their brains and are therefore more powerful than the dinosaur or the saber-tooth tiger. Perhaps the most important period in the history of the earth since the appearance of the first living thing, was when the primates developed so much brain that they could conquer their enemies and get their food better by the use of their intelligence than by the use of their muscles.

Fortune favored the primates, while the ants, the bees, the beavers, the elephants, and the grizzly bears had hard luck. Each in turn developed surprising ability, but for various reasons each failed to conquer the world as the primate has done. In a very amusing little book, *This Simian World*, Clarence Day tries to imagine what this world would have been like if the cat family had won in the contest and had become the supreme animal on the earth. Then in turn he discusses the qualities good and bad of the other great families that might have conquered the earth, such as the elephant family. It is probably good for us to play with these imaginary scenes, for it makes us more appreciative of the excellent characteristics of some of the great animal families, as, for example, the cleanliness of the cat, the patience of the elephant, and what we might call the organizing ability of the ant. Also as we look about us, we then begin to realize that we have certain family traits received from our own great animal family, the primates.

Since we are resting now from that long journey during which we jumped like geological goats from period to period, let us sit cozily on the side of a phantom volcano and imagine another situation.

When the earth was being formed, let us assume that there had formed at the same time one hundred other earths all just like ours. Then let us suppose that microscopic living things had appeared in the warm and shallow water of each of these earths. Do you suppose that a primate would have been developed on each of those hundred earths? If such a queer animal had appeared on each earth, would he have required 1,000 million years to develop in each case as he did on our earth? Of course we don't know, but now that we are resting we can talk it over. Let us each have our own opinion, but you can read mine, for I am writing it here in this book. Of course that does not mean that mine is better than others. And I could be very wrong.

My guess is that not on a single other earth would a primate like us have appeared. On many of those earths animals with brains would have been developed. Perhaps on a few earths the ruling and conquering family of animals would have been much more intelligent than we are. If they should meet us, they might think us crude and savage.

It was only recently that the primates on this earth became so developed that their brains were more powerful than their muscles. Ants and bees developed marvelous brains earlier by 100 million years than we, but while ants nearly succeeded, they nevertheless failed to conquer the world. In some of these other imaginary earths, the ruling family might have developed a brain more powerful than muscles much earlier in their history. Compared with primates on this earth, that early development would give them an immense advantage, so that if we visited such an earth, we would find the ruling family of animals much more civilized than we are.

Since we have become supreme on this earth only after some 1,000 million years of struggle, it is possible that on many of those one hundred imaginary earths, we would find no animal family supreme. Perhaps it would take another interminable age for most of those earths to evolve a family of animals that could really be rulers. In many cases such supremacy might never appear. In perhaps most cases one powerful family might follow another without ever developing an extraordinary amount of brains. We have seen the amphibian succeeded by the reptiles; then came the mammals. In a similar way other earths might have continued until they all became cold and frozen as the sun grew dark.

As time goes on, the leading primates of this earth will probably become both happier and more powerful. By "more powerful" we do not mean that they will build greater navies and taller buildings. We mean that they will know more about themselves and about each other. Then they will become more sensible. They won't quarrel so much with each other, and large groups of primates will seldom fight other large groups in organized war. The primates will learn that by cooperation they can rule the earth more effectively than by fighting among themselves. This ruling of the earth is no easy matter for the primates, for the bacteria that cause disease must be destroyed, and the insects must be prevented from killing our plants and trees.

With more knowledge, greater security, and better health we will probably be happier and more friendly with each other. This being at peace with the other primates on the earth will probably be the most important achievement of all. Apparently such a condition will come only when we have greater knowledge about ourselves and about life in general. The wars and the suffering have been caused in nearly all cases by ignorance. The more intelligent we become, the more informed, the more tolerant we shall be of other people and the more we shall object to the old tendency to get what we want when we want it by killing a number of our enemies and seizing their property.

As the primates continue to add to their vast store of knowledge, they may learn as much about life as they know about electricity.

Of course all this happiness may not come to pass. Perhaps, for aught we know, the sun may grow a little cooler; that is, temporarily so for a few million years. The primates might die as the old dinosaurs did at the end of the Cretaceous Period.

Let us take a more cheerful and also a more probable view. Apparently we are approaching an interglacial period, when in some thousands of years Greenland will have as many forests and flowers as Tennessee now has. Also we are rapidly learning about ourselves and the origin of our customs and ideas. We are becoming less superstitious. Instead of being afraid of the people of another nation we are learning to understand them. Such things tend to make us happier, and they all come from learning more about the earth and the curious animals, including the primates, that live on its surface. If you wish to, you can try to find the answer to a few of those puzzling problems that we have found only half solved as we studied the events of the past.

Some day, when we learn more about the universe, we may find millions of earths among the stars. On tens of thousands of these earths there may be animal families whose brains have become more powerful than their muscles, and some of these families may be very much our superiors. That is a very interesting but a very different subject, so that now, Sam, we must bring to an end the long journey we have taken together down through the geological ages.

Index

DATE DUE

MAR 2 '65			
MAR 22 '65			
MAR 31 '65			
DEC 12 '69			
JAN 7 '70			
JAN 29 '70			
MAR 15 '81			
FEB 3 '98			

PRINTED IN U.S.A.

GAYLORD